PSYCHOANALYSIS
AND
CHRISTIANITY

psychoanalysis
and
christianity

By ARVID RUNESTAM, 1887-

Translated by OSCAR WINFIELD

AUGUSTANA PRESS
ROCK ISLAND, ILLINOIS

PSYCHOANALYSIS AND CHRISTIANITY

Library of Congress Catalog Card Number 58-6526

AUTHOR'S FOREWORD

IT IS now twenty-five years since the first edition of this book was issued. Obviously time has not stood still during these years. But in reality it is astonishing how little has happened in the field covered by this book. An avalanche of psychoanalytical literature has come forth. And Freud's theories have been subjected to rigid criticism. A few of the earlier enthusiasts among Freud's disciples have turned away from psychoanalysis. But the most striking feature is that the argument, at least in so far as it concerns psychoanalysis and the Christian conception of salvation, prances about in the same place. The changes are only variations on the same theme: on the one hand, man is saved only by divine intervention in his life; on the other, man can be saved by his own inner powers, if these powers are brought into proper function by psychoanalysis.

Therefore, this book continues to be timely. However, it has undergone a thorough revision. A new chapter has been added, in which I have aimed at a more definite answer to the problem posed by the book. Chapter VII, Psychoanalytical and Christian

Morality of Adaptation, has been re-written. Moreover, throughout the book, deletions and additions have been made.

Uppsala, Sweden, 1 June, 1957.

ARVID RUNESTAM

TRANSLATOR'S FOREWORD

EVERY age has problems peculiar to itself. That is to say, the physical, political, moral, social, and religious exigencies set up an existential milieu, which may very well solve many problems and answer many questions, while it also poses new problems and asks new questions. This variegated changing pattern inspires hope in some while it fills others with dismay. Among the hopeful are to be found two kinds of persons: the humanist who is sure that the resources of man are sufficient to bring order out of the kaleidoscopic chaos; and the religious person who trusts in a God who is able to cope with the situation, either here and now and/or in a distant future. Among the perplexed and dismayed there are also two kinds of persons: the humanist who may classify himself as an existentialist who finds the raison d'etre in the very restless and unsettled perplexities about him; and the religious person who is sure that the world is evil through and through. There is no hope for it. With detached disdain he turns his back on mundane things and embraces an eschatology which can nurture his hope and give him the nerve needed to withstand the temporary buffeting of everyday living.

It is to be noted that all of these have one thing in common: they are all seeking peace of mind. Whether or not they find it is another matter.

The present turmoil, which may easily be exaggerated, but which cannot be ignored, has greatly increased occasions for anxiety while the means for finding necessary tranquillity or peace of mind have not been augmented. This state of affairs has brought the man of today into a desperate need— need for healing, need for soul cure.

For centuries this need was met more or less successfully by the church, through its services of worship, sacraments, and the private 'ministrations of its pastors. However, during the past several decades, other agencies have come on the scene, agencies that would cast oil upon the troubled waters of the souls of men. The task of the work at hand is to analyze and evaluate this phenomenon.

OSCAR WINFIELD

CONTENTS

I

THE PROBLEM STATED

OUR DAY AND age is in need of healers of the soul. Why is it that modern man turns more readily to other sources of healing for his soul than he does to the church? Is it perhaps that these offer a short cut to salvation which is less demanding than that which the church offers? Or is it that other practitioners of healing really understand modern man better than do the tradition-bound servants of the church?

Yes, I fear that in many instances it is because the others do understand modern man better. If beyond this they are also able to alleviate the conditions calling for correction, and to point out a way less humiliating than that presented by Christian faith, modern man is all the more ready to give heed to what they have to offer.

In any event, it seems to be easier to turn to the physician with one's "bad nerves" than to the pastor with one's spiritual anxiety. The physician looks upon these matters with a greater understanding of human nature. He can afford to be neutral, and to deal with the "case" in an objective manner which is quite different from the procedure of the pastor, and which does not carry with it the implication that the inquirer (patient) is in the presence of moral judgment where he may be found guilty or—what may seem even worse—where he may have to listen to talk about forgiveness. No such embarrassment need be feared in the office of the physician. The psychoanalyst, standing as he does halfway between the physician and the pastor, has undoubtedly profited a great deal from this consideration.

However, another consideration enters in. The scientific claims as well as the implications of truth involved in the very approach of psychoanalysis strike at the very time when the Christian mind is so vacillating as to think that here is the answer to this problem. This claim on the part of psychoanalysis cannot be discounted. Neither may one underestimate the predicament in which the church continually finds itself in this matter. It would be an error indeed, were one to think the danger is past, and that the future is at least theoretically safe. This is far from being the case. Doubt as to the truths of Christianity and its claim to objective data has spread far and wide. Even among people who have no idea of the problems involved in the historical-critical pursuits in this field, including exegetical and general theological problems, one finds deep-rooted skepticism. The whole matter has been cast in a mold of doubt, and for this reason alone the subject has become more or less unapproachable. This may be a sound instinctive reaction; one does not wish to be associated with unreality and self-deceit.

In this turmoil agencies come from every direction proffering salvation on scientific grounds. Here is something experimentally tested and proved; in fact, it rests on psychological theories that claim scientific standing. This is one of the secrets of the success of Christian Science already established, that is, at least for the present time. This procedure is not so much interested in objective facts as it is in the natural and at the same time somewhat mystical healing powers which may be educed and activated from the person's own resources. The same applies to the doctrine of salvation as proclaimed by autosuggestion and, for that matter, of psychoanalysis itself. This salvation, which makes its appeal to nothing beyond the possibilities of man's psychophysical nature, and which does not lay any claim to the greater promises of Christianity, gives the appearance of being founded on the unmovable facts of reality, with the implication that Christianity is not in the same enviable position.

The knowledge which furnishes the background for the message of Christianity does not offer a similar security. This knowledge points to ques-

3

tionable historical facts, and runs into serious conflict with the ordinary demand for truth and reality. He who is sensitive at this juncture will hardly care to proceed further, if this simple demand is not met.

The future of Christianity is dependent on the regaining of a feeling of general security in reference to the character of its reality. Here is a tremendous task which thus presents itself to that systematic Christian knowledge we call *theology*. However, this general faith in the realistic content of Christianity can most certainly not be arrived at through the mere efforts of theology. It is associated with some rather profound repudiations of values centering in life itself; but the task of theology is a link in this profound transformation. Psychoanalysis and all the other methods of salvation reveal by their insistent reference to scientifically established facts that it is paramount for Christian insight to lead men's mind and consciousness to a renewed confidence in the truth of Christianity and the objective reality with which it deals. A distinction between religion and theology, however fine, must never be so applied as to obfuscate the meaning and function of theology.

Now, the manner in which the truth-aspect of Christianity may establish itself is quite another matter. In this connection real significance becomes attached to the query as to whether theology has anything to learn from psychoanalysis. According to my understanding at this point, theology has a great deal to learn. I am convinced of this because of the reference made by psychoanalysis to "Tiefenpsychologie," a psychology which aims to reach the deepest levels of the human soul. It is not quite certain that psychoanalysis is able to reach down to this level; but it has at least posed a problem for theology. The problem or task here involved is to seek psychologically to give moorings to the eternal values and verities by a more profound penetration of the prerequisites set by the human soul. The expression must not be misunderstood. It does not imply that Christian salvation should be a process confined only to the "psyche," in such a manner as to make revelation superflous. On the contrary, "the eternal" must be so grounded psychologically that it becomes apparent that the acts of life which alone give life its real meaning cannot be achieved without the vitalizing, ennobling, and normative power generated by revelation.

In the sifting process through which the historical element in Christianity is now passing one finds one of the promising signs of our time in this, that psychology as such and, in addition, psychoanalysis are pointing to *basic human nature*. This is so because in a certain sense it may be said that theology, and especially the historical aspects of Christianity, may be safeguarded by the mooring of the eternal verities in nature, that is, in a "natural theology." This must not be construed to mean that saving power lies in something given in man's nature, but rather that that which is the given in man's nature is such that it unconditionally demands the saving power of an objective revelation in order that this human nature may find its real meaning. And this to such a degree that the most profoundly "natural" actions of man cannot come to be without the intervention of a revelatory power in human life. But what this power "reveals" and permits man to "see" must be such that it awakens not only the functions of the mind, that is his reason, but also those of his heart, his will, and his total personality. What is implicit here must be made explicit by the following qualification: the only revelation that can be of help in man's striving for a meaning of life consonant with his real nature is that revelation which unveils to the extent that it liberates one for new vistas of life on the one hand, and liberates the very spirit of man from the fetters of his preoccupation with himself on the other.

In this sense theology must become "natural theology." It is for theology to attempt to show that man under the conditions of faith and love primarily finds himself in a "natural" situation. Everything else is unnatural. Only the freedom of God's image to develop its powers in the sunshine of grace is true nature. From this theological position psychoanalysis, with its "Tiefenpsychologie," also has the right to be considered. The question is this, however: Considering its psychological presuppositions, does it possess the possibilities necessary to find this *eternally natural?* Opinions on this matter can be given only after we have better learned to know its methodology and general approach. Theology at this juncture desires nothing more than clarity in regard to the genius, content, and truth of the Christian faith and life. And anything that may help to further this clarity it must greet with joy. Moreover, according to my conception, theology must give very special attention and anticipation to that young science called psychology, and to the new gains made by it in psychoanalysis.

From another point of view it should be noted that psychology is really nothing new as far as theology is concerned. It follows that theology should not now, any more than at any previous time, run to some other science for information as to what resides in man, simply because this new science advertises itself as a specialist in this field. Theology has in its own right practiced psychology too long to allow itself to take orders from outside sources as to the inner life of the soul. Christian theology has its own psychology, its own anthropology, and its own conception of man's essence and basic constitution. Psychoanalysis and Christianity: this is not only psychology versus theology; it is also *psy-*

chology versus psychology. This is what is absolutely decisive in any debate (or discussion) between psychoanalysis and Christianity. When, therefore, modern psychic research proffers its services to theology, then theology may very well ask whether or not the new psychology actually agrees with its own psychology; if it really helps it better to clarify its own content, or if it just obfuscates something which is essential to itself; but surely it must also ask itself if theology may not need to correct its own psychology in the face of the findings of the new psychology. The duty of self-examination is paramount for both sides; and surely with mutual benefit.

The consideration just suggested applies particularly to psychoanalysis. The latter is a phenomenon which, both as to theory and practice, is not yet stable. Not only is it divided into several opposing camps; it is also frequently obscure as to the implications of its methodology, its resources, and the scope of its validity. At one time it may construct a cause and effect psychological outlook, and pass as a natural science; at another it subjects life to a teleological frame of reference, and aims to *understand*, to disclose meanings, and in this way to serve as guide; all this in addition to mere psychological clarification.

Again, it may embrace the whole of life and seek to make all things clear as well as offer panaceas for all ailments. Or it may assure one that it tolerates and needs other services to come to its aid, which services it would otherwise dismiss as needless. Obviously psychoanalysis must come to its senses and arrive at a modicum of stability, if it would become usable. And least of all would it fail to benefit from taking cognizance of Christianity with its nearly two thousand years of tried and tested psychology and practice. This would apply all the more, since psychoanalysis itself is an activity which in theory and practice moves about in an area which appears at least to be the same as that of Christian theory and practice.

This practical alignment on the part of psychoanalysis carries with it, by the way, something of extraordinary importance in its simulation of Christianity; it cannot in this respect escape the necessity of dealing with something psychically *normal*. This is not contradicted by the fact that psychoanalysis is frequently accused of reaching out too far, paying too much attention to, and building too much upon, psychopathological phenomena. However this may be, even if psychoanalysis has been censured justly because it has all too often received its concepts of normality and "the natural" from the abnormal and the unnatural, it is nevertheless true that it has kept in mind a notion of normality within the framework under consideration. Psychoanalysis, as well as Christianity, does really have an ideal as to health. It conducts its diagnosis, engages in its practice, and finally gives its pedagogical directions in reference to its concept of what is normally human. Obviously this must be the case, because when one deals with the psychically or spiritually abnormal for the purpose of making correction, one must presuppose the presence of a notion of what is normal.

Both psychoanalysis and Christianity, by their efforts, desire to achieve health for the soul. Both would "redeem from evil." But, in the very conception of what the evil is from which one is to be saved, the antithesis between them becomes obvious. Of course, this is not strange. And ordinarily, per se, this would not be of much concern to a Christian. There are, after all, so many kinds of evil. And Christianity cannot very well look askance if other agencies engage against evils with which it cannot cope or against those that lie in the periphery of its functions. For this reason Christianity has never, where it has sensed its function rightly, thought of medical science as a competitor.

As a matter of fact, psychoanalysis, as to its genesis, is a medical phenomenon; that is, from the start it has been a medical practice with a medical technique. In its beginnings it no doubt gave its attention only to the more serious ailments—acute hysteria, acute compulsion-psychoneuroses, etc. Thus far it had no occasion of consequence to come into conflict with Christianity any more than did general medical science. To be sure, circumstances surrounding it at the very beginning tended to bring it closer to the scene of action occupied by Christianity, since both considered man's psyche their object of interest.

In any case, from a Christian point of view there has been no desire to deny that even the soul can, strictly speaking, be ill in a medical sense, and thus stand in need of medical care. It is precisely for this reason we have our asylums, psychiatrists, and nerve specialists. At this juncture the relationship between pastor and physician has been characterized by mutual understanding. But even in the case of purely physical, organic diseases, the mind is a factor and varies considerably with bodily changes. This fact cannot be ignored by the physician. Thus, along the whole line one finds the work of pastor and physician encountering each other. This is nothing new. It has ever been thus, or it was so in every instance long before psychoanalysis came into being.

However, something new has entered in. From the moment psychoanalysis began to broaden its field of activity and make claims that it may be applied not only to the more serious cases of psychopathology, cases which belong to or border on insanity, but also to the "milder" cases, which belong in the area of religion and the pastor's general practice, it began to assume the cure of souls in a very real sense. And it is with such claims and ambitions that psychoanalysis is now stepping forth. The modern soul-healing psychoanalyst frequently claims the right to take the place of the pastor. Freud himself envisioned public institutions for psychoanalysis, where not only a few well to do, but where the great masses might have access to the blessings of the art of psychotherapy. And others have more directly copied his method and applied it in the direction of a general soul cure which in a certain measure appears as a competitor of Christian pastoral soul cure.

It is from these broadened claims on the part of psychoanalysis that I here take my departure. The circumstances being what they are, one is entitled to opine: If now the psychoanalyst is to assume the role of giving pastoral care, he will have to deal with essentially the same problems as those that have always confronted the pastor—that is, unless man suddenly has become transformed and operates with other basic needs, desires, and instincts from those with which he formerly operated.

Now among psychoanalysts with a more balanced outlook it is acknowledged that not all soul cure requires or must have psychoanalytical treatment, and that one should select and treat those among the mentally maladjusted who lend themselves to this form of healing. But even under such considerations one finds it difficult to draw the line between religio-moral problems of the mind which should be dealt with by Christian pastoral care and other mental ills. Yes, day by day it becomes more obvious to the psychoanalyst himself that the conflicts with which he must deal in the final analysis are of a moral or religio-moral nature. Actually there is always a conscience conflict to be found in the distress of the soul; that is, a feeling of guilt, a feeling which demands punishment and expiation. Were one to survey the claims of psychoanalysts, by and large, it would in every case be obvious that there is no intention on their part to differentiate and segregate cases that may be designated as religio-moral spiritual pathology. Obviously psychoanalysis does not desire to abdicate the right to treat even the most profoundly serious spiritual conflicts.

On the other hand, it has broadened its conception of the type of mental ailments suitable for psychoanalytic treatment so as to include not only extreme cases of neurosis and hysteria, or the clearly demarcated distress of a religio-moral order, but also the nervousness and the anxiety which appear as a kind of general human pathology which, so it is implied, really leave no family and hardly any contemporary person quite untouched. This is especially accentuated in the present-day anagogical approach represented by certain schools of psychoanalysis.

Thus psychoanalysis does not refrain from the treating of a given case of mental distress simply because moral factors and a sense of guilt are involved, any more than a sensible pastor would turn away a person suffering spiritually simply because no sense of guilt is consciously present in his distress. Were the servants of the church to relieve themselves of responsibility for that large number of the spiritually ill who are not pressed by a conscious sense of guilt, and leave the matter in the hands of other soul healers, they would most certainly simplify their assignment. The implication here has references to the following observation: It can most certainly be established that distress of soul has for some time and to a great extent actually not appeared as a conscious sense of guilt nor as moral distress. This marks the change that has taken place in this matter. *The sense of guilt has declined, but there is no corresponding change in spiritual distress. The sense of guilt has declined, but neuroticism has increased.* The latter "has become the festering sores of our time,"[1] just to cite one psychoanalyst; it is "a common human ailment (folk-sjukdom) and there is danger that the race may degenerate," states another.[2] The sense of guilt has frequently transformed itself into an uncertain anguish.

If in this unfortunate status of the soul there is a hidden sense of guilt, and if, according to the

14

usual conception of the matter, it is judged to belong, in the strictest sense, to the area of pastoral care, then the pastor is given a more meticulous assignment.

This means, of course, that one cannot heedlessly approach a person laden with anguish with a sermon concerning sin and guilt and forgiveness, and thus force upon him a sense of guilt that is beyond his power to contain. In general, the following rule is an excellent guide in pastoral care: "The rule that it is improper to force, or even impatiently to make an effort to extract, a resolving of a psychical and/or moral conflict." "Each soul is a case by itself, and must be understood and judged according to its own possibilities, not according to some catechism"[3] It is thus a matter of taking the person as he is with his frequently uncertain anguish and his worry and his questions which may seem trivial, but on which his pathologic mind has taken a strong hold, and lead on to the really sensitive point, whatever it may be. As surely as, according to evangelical Christianity, sin and guilt are at the core of all anguish, just as surely, nevertheless, may "salvation from evil" be looked upon not only as atonement, but also as a delivery from evil; that is, as being set free, not only from guilt but also from other temporal suffering and woe; not only from the pangs of conscience, but also from the despair resulting from meaninglessness, hopelessness, and

15

emptiness. It may, however, occur, and even on this the pastor must center his attention, that behind indefinite suffering and agony of soul, there is a hidden conscience factor, hidden from others and half-hidden from the sufferer himself. For the trained pastor this holds no secret. He is not, therefore, surprised when he finds that the psychoanalyst has made the same discovery in reference not only to the "spiritual distress" which seeks out the pastor, but also the "neuroticism" which turns to the neurologist. In this matter, however, it is possible that the Christian pastor may have an idea quite different from that of the psychoanalyst as to how this sense of guilt in itself is to be considered. Is it something which at the same time as it is an "evil" is a normal, sound reaction? Or as a pathological phenomenon? Or there may be a third possibility: may it be possible to differentiate between a normal, "healthy" sense of guilt, and one that is abnormal and pathological?

The problem comes to a point in these queries. And right here the Christian pastor is confronted by extraordinary difficulties. Actually he is not in a position to refuse his services to anyone in spiritual need simply because the person in question does not seem to him to possess the proper indications of a penitent attitude. There must of necessity be the pain of compassion in his heart whenever one such, seeking help, must needs depart without his succor. If analysis proffers means better able to give aid, and more inclusive aid, he must not close that door before him.

It is unthinkable that any need that comes to his attention should be estranged from his love. Does not the gospel demand this of him? He must, however, take care not to overestimate his own powers in view of the need that confronts him. And this may very well be applied to such need as the conscious sense of guilt. This may appear in such a form that not the pastor but the physician is the proper person to engage against it. Even if, as the Danish chief physician Schou contends, something like the melancholic's sickly sense of guilt reveals something constitutive in human life, in other words, is *normal* to the extent that it uncovers a genuine natural element in man, and sickly only to the extent that it appears in a distorted form, this distortion is nevertheless enough to cause the minister to stand nonplussed, and need the help of the physician. It is quite possible that the prime need for him who comes and complains about his evil or his heavy heart is not phrases about the forgiveness of sins but rather the physician's prescription to the effect that he take to his bed for a needed rest. To speak to him in Christian terminology would be as out of place as to offer the Gospel of Jesus to one hard pressed by strictly material needs. It just does not work. He needs to be relieved from something else first, before the more serious trouble, the sorrow which is according to the mind of God, can get firm hold of his soul. The same is undoubtedly true in reference to diseases of a nervous order. And if the pastor is to concern himself with such cases, he must of necessity accept the person just as he is, and not anticipate the events.

Obviously, then, a given case is not more suitable for treatment in terms of the Christian evangel simply because it involves a sense of guilt. Cases of this sort have already come before physicians of mental hospitals and neurologists with the implication that no pastoral aid is necessary. And the psychoanalyst is said to be less inclined to turn over these cases to the pastor. If the psychoanalyst would be willing, in a general way, to join in the making of a line of demarcation between his practice and that of the pastor, that line would obviously be where he would reserve for himself all cases involving "suppression." With this we have arrived at the point in our presentation which demands that we make further acquaintance with the theory and practice of psychoanalysis.

My points of departure have been as follows: First I have considered the broadened claims of psychoanalysis, claims which have tended toward a general soul cure by means of which the analyst has begun to emerge as a competitor of the pastor as the spiritual healer of souls. Secondly, I have noted that psychoanalysis refers to a general nervousness of our day as a disease especially characteristic of contemporary man, a disease that requires the service of psychoanalysis.

A third and final point of departure centers around the role played by the sense of guilt in nervous disorders. I combine this with the immediately preceding observation, and from this emerges the following query: What is the place and basis for the sense of guilt in the spiritual anxiety which manifests itself in the widespread nervous disorders? This problem forces me to enter into an examination of the theory and technique of psychoanalysis with special attention to its doctrine of repression. The result from this inquiry will then be applied to cases in point and to the present situation; and in this manner it is aimed to meet the objections made by psychoanalysis in its accusation that morality is needlessly strict. In this connection it will also become apparent to what extent the anxiety and corresponding sense of guilt emerging from modern nervous disorders are symptomatic of disease or health. Following this confrontation between psychoanalysis and morality, I shall inquire into the position of psychoanalysis in reference to religion, and by contrastive juxtaposition I shall compare the liberation offered by psychoanalysis and that presented by Christian salvation in order, finally, to dwell on the ultimate presuppositions and differences between Christian and psychoanalytical psychology, including the ethical implications and a general philosophy of life.

NOTES AND REFERENCES

[1] Johs. Irgens Strömme: *Nervösitet*, pp. 9, 13. Cf. E. Wexberg: *Individualpsychologie*, p. 205 f.

[2] Iwan Bratt: *Kultur och nevros*, p. 112.

[3] Tor Andrae: *Psychoanalys och religion*, p. 67.

II.

THE ESSENTIAL FEATURES OF THE THEORY AND PRACTICE OF PSYCHOANALYSIS. "REPRESSION"

As a basis for the following presentation I shall give a brief account of the chief characteristics of the theory and technique of psychoanlysis, placing special emphasis on those phases which may be of value for the point of view I intend to pursue. I hope to be able to do so without the necessity of going into further detail in reference to the various trends and theories of psychoanalysis.

The closest precursor of the psychoanalytical method is the principle of catharsis, applied by Breuer and Freud. This method depended on hypnosis. By hypnosis the patient was reduced to a psychic state in which the symptom appeared for the first time. "Then, in the hypnotized person, emerged memories, thoughts, and impulses which before had been absent from his consciousness and when he, under intensive emotional strain, managed to communicate the mental course of events to his physician, the symptom was overcome and its return suppressed."[1]

But Freud undertook to change this method of

catharsis when he developed his psychoanalytical method to the extent that he gave up hypnosis. "At the present time he treats his patients in such a manner that he, without any other influence on them, lets them lie comfortably on a couch, while he places himself out of sight on a chair behind them. He does not ask them to close their eyes, and he avoids contact with them, as he avoids any procedure that might involve hypnosis. Thus, a session of this sort proceeds as a conversation between two persons equally awake." In this manner it is possible for a larger number of people to be given psychoanalytic treatment, since by far not all people are susceptible to hypnosis. For the help offered by hypnosis in reaching the delicately tender spot, Freud finds compensation in the following. He encourages the patient to surrender himself to increasingly free association, to allow thoughts and words to come and go freely, and to speak whatever comes to mind without concern as to coherence. Above all, he exhorts him not to exclude anything because it seems embarrassing or otherwise painful. In that process the patient is more than likely to enter into an account of his illness.

As a matter of course, in this connection the analyst discovers gaps, irregularities, failure of memory, and lack of continuity in the story; and these are of special interest to him. He seeks to fill these gaps, but finds resistance, and this resistance must be overcome. Gaps in memory have arisen because psychic forces have repressed a certain mental content and, as it were, stand on guard at the entrance to the scene of memory. A certain psychic content has been suppressed into the subconscious—to what purpose and by which forces we shall soon see. That which has been included in the subconscious, and which the psychoanalyst desires to reach, is not dead and inactive, however; it "lies in wait, looking for an opportunity to be activated, and is then capable of presenting a deformed and unrecognizable compensatory notion in place of that which has been suppressed in the conscious mind—hence the symptom."[2] To penetrate into the enclosed and subconscious and bring it into the open, through these peculiar and symbolical expressions is thus the assignment accepted by psychotherapy.

It is, therefore, important to interpret these symbols correctly, and by these means to penetrate into the world of the subconscious. The patient's fancies, dreams, unintentional and unplanned actions, slips of the tongue, etc., may be regarded as such symbols. When, through these interpretations of symbols, the gaps in memory have been filled, the opposition broken, the suppressions liberated and the unconscious made conscious, the cure is completed and in the best cases the patient restored to health.

A matter of considerable importance is the fact that the analyst seems to be unable to reach the cause for the repression without the aid of that phenomenon called "transference." This is the second factor of prime importance in the analytical liberation process, and it is essentially an emotional factor. The patient transfers his "feeling" to the analyst, and makes him an object of strong emotional attachment, often mixed with or replaced by feelings of hostility. With his physician he relives the experience, including its emotional strain, which earlier was the genesis of the repression which in turn produced the illness. In the intellectual and technical clarification of the neurosis for the conscious, the transfer enters in as a more personal factor and one which accentuates the importance of personal feelings involved in the process of release. Being bound to the analyst makes it possible for the emotions to break loose and set themselves in motion. When the process of cure has advanced sufficiently, it becomes necessary for the analyst to set the patient free from this dependence, and to direct his emotions to some other object upon which he can expend his energy in a wholesome manner.

Thus, psychoanalysis is also psychotherapy, a practical and technical method for the healing of the souls of men, and also, indirectly a method for the healing of strictly bodily ailments which have their origin in the focalized pathology of the soul. However, psychoanalysis as psychotherapy has undergirded itself with a psychological theory— just the same as Christianity, as a practical proclamation of salvation and practice of soul cure, has been eager to get support from a doctrine of God, man, and the world. In this manner, psychoanalysis has become "the new psychology."

What is it, then, that makes the new psychology new as a science about the mind? It is that it has directed its attention to the "unconscious," or the "subconscious." Strictly speaking, so psychoanalysis implies, only a small fraction of what occurs in the mind actually emerges into the daylight of the conscious; the major portion lies in the dark or twilight of the subconscious. But it is not inactive; it plays a role of extraordinary significance in giving dynamic form to the life, thinking, feeling, will, and action of the conscious mind. Psychology as such has no right, claims the new psychology, to disregard this world of the subconscious; above everything else, it deserves our attention, since it is from this, in such a large measure, that our emotions have their origin, and from which our thoughts, will, and action get their directives.

I cannot here enter into a discussion concerning the varying theories about the different strata of the subconscious. What interests us here primarily is the so-called Freudian unconscious, the repressed unconscious. That it is repressed does not mean, as has already been intimated, that it is inactive or of no influence. On the contrary, in the unconscious it performs a subterranean task with ominous import, and is able, so to speak, to transpose life into a different key. Neither does it remain totally hidden in the unconscious, but emerges from time to time in the sphere of the conscious, but always in deformed shapes and in isolated phases, not quite understandable. Especially in the case of dreams, where resistance is lowered, the repressed unconscious comes to the surface. Moreover, this may also occur in unguarded moments, in slips of speech, in thoughtless actions and gestures. In such situations a person may easily betray himself and reveal that there is a repressed content which can be kept hidden only with considerable effort; not a conscious, but an unconscious effort.

What is significant in reference to the supressed unconscious is that it is an *evil;* e. g., it is something which the ego has been unable to accept and assimilate, but something which of necessity it has had to drive aside, drive away, forget, deny because of its opposition to its interest. It may be something quite innocent, a meaningless event which has gone against our feelings, which has involved humiliation or something similar. But it may also concern serious matters. In general, one may say that this evil focus of repressed mental content results when a wish impulse is checked in its course and is not suppressed or sidetracked and sublimated, e. g., when it cannot, either in gross or refined form, follow through, but is repressed. The term "repress" expresses simply a conflict which is not resolved but is pushed aside and is, as it were, reserved for the future, is "forgotten." As intimated, it does not mean that the drive in question is actually *suppressed*, or that its energy is put to use by a stronger force, but it implies a certain secret accumulation of hidden energy, because "in the unconscious the suppressed wish-fulfillment remains."[3] "Freud's great discovery is that neuroses and their symptoms are nourished largely by energy from sex desires which have not been successfully suppressed. This failure of attempted suppression has had the result that of these desires nothing, or only isolated parts, can be found in the conscious mind, while at the same time, their total energy, or at least the greater portion thereof, continually remains operative in the subconscious, that is to say, operative in a more or less withdrawn part of the soul under the influence of the conscious ego."[4]

There may be various impulse compensations which in this manner may effect the process of repression and form a basis for repressed unconscious image representations, characterized by exaggerated feelings and loaded emotions. This congeries of factors and processes has been given the name "complex." More accurately stated: There are differences of opinion among psychoanalysts about the correct interpretation of the *urdrift,* or basic drive,

27

which it is thought controls man, the checking of which is the ultimate occasion for the formation of repression. That is to say, man's inner life is beheld in the image of a stream of life, or several such streams, which flow with something of the necessity of natural powers, and is restrained or forced to assume other courses, or forces hindrances out of its way.[5]

In the following paragraphs I shall demonstrate that in the view of life reflected by this picture, there is a "philosophy of life" in disguise, however much psychoanalysis itself may deny this. As has been said, however, varying contents are attributed to this stream of life ("livsström") by different psychoanalysts. As is known, Freud identifies it with the sex drive, libido, although he strives to give it a broader content than a mere sex drive. At times he therefore also speaks of "psychosexuality" and says: "We use the word sexuality in the same inclusive meaning as that of the German word 'lieben.' "[6] The sense and logic Freud employs thus to "spiritualize" sexuality will be more closely investigated in the chapter on "Sublimation."

Freud himself attaches the neurosis producing conflicts, bound up with the basic sex drive, to childhood; to the so-called Oedipus frustration. This is the situation: The sex instinct plays an important role already in the earliest years of childhood, although it is essentially tied up with other organs

28

and projects toward objects other than those of the mature sex drive. Its earliest expression is evidenced in suckling at the mother's breast. The very act of suckling becomes a satisfying of the child's innate drive (lustbehov) or libido. Even the evacuation of the bowels is said to have a similar meaning for the infant. When later the conditions and realities of life render these expressions of the libido impossible or meaningless, autoeroticism sets in, when the child makes his own body the subject-object for the satisfaction of his desires. Following this there is the period of "incestuousness," the period of the Oedipus complex, when the child's libido is directed towards its parents.

Thus it is the sexual instinct that attaches the child to its parents. But the attachment of the male child is quite different from that of the female. The male child through his sex instinct is overwhelmingly attached to the mother; similarly, the female child to the father, even if a sexual relationship of a contrary order obtains, or as a rule appears to be the case. This bond can become a cause of neurosis only if a normal release does not take place at the right time. If this does not occur, so that the infantile inhibition, by means of repression, remains in the unconscious of the adult, this remainder from childhood becomes the occasion for mental conflict and neurosis. As far as Freud is concerned, the repressed sexual instinct directed towards the parents becomes the core complex of every neurosis. The process of repression thus begins quite early. Under the influence of nurture and general rearing, even before the age of puberty, extremely potent repressions have taken place, and mental forces such as a sense of shame, loathing, and moral sense have arisen, which act as censors and support these repressions. These restraining forces later attain considerably greater importance when the drives become even more powerful in the age of puberty.

A presupposition for repression is, in every case, a conflict between two drives or two mental forces in man. This conflict, according to Freud, is one between the principle of lust on the one hand and the principle of reality on the other. Lust is the more primitive. "In the beginning was lust!" But in the history of the race as well as that of the individual, the principle of reality, with its demands, has set itself up against lust. It did no permit man to give himself over to lust. It forced man to insure his existence, to provide for his preservation, to bow before the inevitable and make his adjustments. In the process other drives came into being. The ego drives came into competition with the sex drive. And it is these ego drives or this "I" that comes to the fore in the suppression of the demands of the sex drive. But the greatest and most dangerous force of this "I" comes about when it assumes the form of the "superego," or moral ego which it develops in its confrontation with "reality." It is finally obvious that this is what causes the dangerous conflict.[7]

The conflict may be resolved in many ways; it may even be so resolved that no repression need occur. But it may also be resolved, or more correctly speaking, *be postponed* through repression: one of the forces is shut off from normal access to the conscious, and is preserved with its emotional content in the unconscious; "it is forgotten," "it is disassociated" from the essential consciousness, without at the same time being destroyed and made to cease its underground activity.

The emotions which are attached to these repressed complexes are, thus, emotions of utter disgust. It is for this reason they carry with them disastrous consequences for mental health.

However, the unconscious has also another aspect, which has been strongly accentuated by other tendencies within psychoanalysis, but which later have come into their own right even with Freud himself. The unconscious needs to include not only a repressed "evil" but also a "good." At times, as in Scandinavian psychoanalysis, the unconscious good is elevated to divine rank and is compared to divine grace, which grace also operates "subconsciously," without any conscious effort of our own. This good is actually the overflowing "life-interest" itself, the libido, most forcefully expressed or symbolized in sexual potency. This love drive or ecstatic verve becomes evil only as it is *repressed,* "confined," that is, hindered by some opposing force from free access to the function of giving form and meaning to life.

It is the repression, then, that causes the pathological *nervous* state. Technically this pathology can now also be determined. I quote a definition by Em. af Geijerstam: "Were one to offer a definition of neuroses, one might say that he is a neurotic who does not possess what one could call a complete adjustment to life, that is to say, one who is without full devotion to life and its demands and—well worth noting—its consequences."[8] In other words he is a neurotic, the function of whose ecstatic drive has been checked. And today there are so many nervous people because so many suffer from just such restraint. In certain areas within psychoanalysis there has been a predisposition to engage in a general diagnosis of the present-day mind and culture. Thus in so far as the state of nervousness has been found to be a constitutional aspect in the soul of contemporary man, it has also been implied that the conflict causing neuroses has been brought about in this manner: the modern civilized community with its mores and morality has set up too high a standard for a released expression of the instincts, and has restrained a free functioning of the libido, the ecstascy drive, and the spontaneous, naive passion for living. For example, the difficulty in our modern community to enter into early matrimony and set up a normal home life is one of the central sources for neurosis. Again, the restrictive bonds which the school in many ways places upon the growing generation are another source. And if the community and its laws had not placed hindrances in the way, the constraint of the mores and morality would have hindered normal overt functions of the drives involved. Thus in many instances the emotions are forced to the lowest level where a center of mental disquietude is set up.

These considerations pose the question as to the moral quality involved in nervous anxiety. We shall now proceed to a closer examination of this state of affairs.

NOTES AND REFERENCES

[1] Freud: *Gesammelte Schriften,* Vol. VI, p. 3 f.

[2] Ibid., Vol. IV, p. 371.

[3] Freud: *Ges. Schr.,* Vol. IV, p. 371.

[4] Muller-Braunschweig: *Das Verhältnis der Psychoanalyse zu Etwik, Religion und Seelsorge. Arzt u Seelsorger,* Vol. 11, 1927, p. 35.

[5] Cf. Tansley: *Den nya psykologien,* p. 64.

[6] *Ges. Schr.,* Vol. VI, p. 39.

[7] In the next chapter I shall return to a discussion of this moral factor involved in suppression.

[8] *Zur Frage des Verdrangungsproblems. Acta psychiatria et neruologica,* Vol. II, Frasc. 1, 1927, p. 7.

III

NEUROTICISM AND MORALITY

"THROUGH MANY YEARS of investigation," says
Pfister, "it has become evident that the majority of
the deepest repressions have come about in the face
of some ethical conflict."[1] "The process of repression is associated with a potent moral will which is
met by a forceful counterwill having the nature of
a drive."[2] "It is namely," states Bjerre, "not sexuality in and of itself which causes illness in men,
but the struggle against it and therewith a struggle
against themselves, into which they are forced due
to moral demands; and similar valuations get the
lion's share of their power from the undertones and
prejudices of religion."[3] The profoundest repressions include also a sense of guilt, an unconscious
sense of guilt and an unconscious need for punishment. This unconscious sense of guilt "compels us"
states Franz Alexander, "practically to accept a
mental authority which reacts with a sense of guilt
upon certain unconscious emotions and judges them
as it would many actions under a conscious conscience. Thus this authority evaluates wishes,
thoughts, in brief, psychical data or facts, as if they

were actions. It operates in the same manner as does the conscious judgment, with the exception that its whole action in the process of selection and censorship occurs in the unconscious."[4]

What is now this moral authority? Alexander replies: "Psychoanalytical experience shows us that the moral lines of direction in this authority are identical with the prohibitions and commands which the child in its early years receives from its parents. On the other hand, the investigation of this authority evokes certain phylogenetical reminiscences from man's primitive history. This lawbook, submerged in the unconscious, is as to its essence identical to the totemistic lawbook of primitive people. Its chief prohibition is directed against the male's incestuous desire, and against feelings of enmity toward the father. In this authority we must, therefore, see the result of its preparation throughout the history of the species, and through education its established adaptation to the social needs and laws which make up the foundations for contemporary community organization. The contribution in question is a product of adaptation, 'ein domestizierter sozial gewordener Teil des Ichs,' designated by Freud as the superego. It is very closely related to repression. Freud takes for granted that a large share of the repressions are undertaken by this ego under the influence of this social authority. The psychoanalytical investigation of neurotics demonstrates to us, with tedious monotony, that wishes and tendencies which in the first place are victims of repression and later arrive at symbolization are simply those that gainsay the lawbook of the super-ego," consequently, the moral code of this subconsciously operating moral authority.

The morality that is active in the ego or the superego thus receives the dubious honor of being the repressing factor in the process of repression that leads to neurosis. And because the censoring moral ego functions unconsciously to a large extent, it originates an unconscious sense of guilt and an unconscious demand for punishment.

From the standpoint of mental health, the suppressed unconscious must be evaluated as an *evil*. Suppression is not a normal resolving of conflict. This quality of being something evil, therefore, also imparts that which is repressed to the *repressing factor*. However necessary the moral censor may be admitted to be, psychoanalysis gives its special attention to the fact that it produces repression, and for this reason plays a devastating role in reference to mental health. Pfister says: "Conscience is of the greatest importance to moral life. But its danger lies in its tendency to create repression instead of simple mastery. *The more strictly it judges, the greater is the danger of repression.*"[5]

The psychoanalytic theory about repression, and the widespread neuroses based thereon, therefore give the total impression of a strong rancor on the part of psychoanalysis toward the needlessly strict censure of the life drive by contemporary morality.[6] Moreover, individual trends of thought in related areas make no effort to remove this general impression. Psychoanalysis stands forth both in theory and practice, by and large, as a potent promoter of the right of the spontaneous instinct-guided life to make itself effective. It is not as if it means that all morality is evil per se. But morality presents itself more as a necessary evil than as a positive good. Conscience and the "superego" receive the role of operating purely negatively and restrictively on that which alone appears to possess the right to life, "the life stream" itself.[7]

The concept which psychoanalysis has in reference to morality, namely, that it is the most potent factor in repression, agrees with its theory about the genesis and manifestation of morality. Essentially it is looked upon as a product of training, a point of social adaptation, and at last, if one may believe Freud, something with an economic implication. "The community must, of course, among its most important functions of education include the harnessing and restricting of the sex drive, and subject it to an individual will, which must be identical to the social command, that is, when this drive breaks through as a drive of propagation . . . The motive of human society is, in the final analysis, economic: when the means of livelihood is not sufficient to support its members without their labor, it must limit the number of people and direct their energies away from sexual activity to (productive) labor."[8] How one can explain the genesis of the mores in the concepts of psychoanalysis, under these conditions, as Pfister tries to do, is quite impossible to understand.

In the following chapters I shall show the validity of my analysis of the intentions which govern psychoanalysis at this point. This is not something which for the first time in history has directed itself against "the law." There are other movements antedating it which have won recognition in like manner. We need only to reflect on Luther's struggle against the law and his vivid experience of how the law can become a genuine devil in one's conscience, in order that we may not further make ourselves misunderstood in the presence of the solicitous attitude on the part of psychoanalysis about frustration of the energy of life or love. That which seemingly lies nearest at hand, however, when, from a Christian point of view one must look askance at the theory of psychoanalysis, is to pose this query: With what justice does it throw suspicion on moral authority and with what justice, in reference to the general nervousness of today, does it blame morality for excessive strictness and rigorous censure? But, first and foremost, the doctrine of repression itself, and the operative forces of its processes, must be subjected to a closer scrutiny.

That to which psychoanalysis, with its doctrine of repression, has called our attention is not something entirely unknown to literature. Especially here, as in so many other ways, fiction has preceded scientific psychological investigation. Frequently one finds references to Shakespeare's "Macbeth" and Ibsen's "Fruen fra havet," as examples of fiction's comprehension of the power of unconscious suppression in people's lives. But the honor of having directed scientific research to this matter accrues entirely to psychoanalysis. And it is without a doubt a deserved honor. Least of all should theology be slow in giving unreserved recognition to this, if for no other reason than that the *subject matter itself* is not in the least strange. The whole concept, that something broods in the recesses of the soul, something which is repressed, something probably cut off from *direct* effectiveness, but which by the rear entrance forces itself into our conscious feeling, willing, and active life is, of course, really an old and well known line of thought as far as Christianity is concerned. That there are forces at work in the depths of the subconscious—forces of both good and evil—independent of man's free choice, intellect, and power is, in any case, nothing which was strange to the greatest characters in Christian history, even if they did not, like psychoanalysis, stop with the exclusively human in their apprehension of the mysterious power of good and evil, but rather restored it to superhuman wills.

But the fact of repression obviously seems to be easily verifiable in anyone's general experience. Practically, it may be taken for granted that all of us have in some measure become acquainted with repression, perhaps in its coarser forms: I mean we have given some evidence of "repression" of the claims of certain innate powers, which have never been completely satisfied on the one hand, or completely rejected on the other, the implication being that these powers have never been remolded into a more precious metal but remain in the secret recesses in all their crudeness. In our dealing with people we have, perchance, had the experience at times when it seemed as if a subterranean world opens up in their inner being; a world which gives one the impression that it is kept secret not only from others but also from the person himself. It may be a closed-in bitterness, some jealousy, or a desire for revenge which escapes in an unguarded moment; or some basic innate characteristic gushing forth, betraying deep-felt grievance and repressed depravity. Not a word need be expressed; it may very well be simply a gesture or a look by a person in an unguarded moment, who himself at the time feels free from observation and for this reason can afford to ease up on the strenuous watchfulness which he, often unconsciously, must maintain over his own vital, robust, sensual but repressed drives of one kind or another. That such a postponed and probably half-forgotten arrangement between the moral ego and nagging wishes and drives of another kind can make a person nervous and insecure in the course of his life is sufficiently exemplified. And most assuredly can this state of affairs lead us to suspect the possibility of even more deeply imbedded and more mysterious processes of repression, with concomitant neurotic structuration.

However, there are two objections to the psychoanalytical doctrine of repression. These, by the way, finally unite into one. With reference to the notion that it is primarily the sex instinct and the emotional energy it involves, which the analysts imply have been unduly restrained, one may ask: As one looks at the present situation and the contemporary moral condition, is there anything that seems to indicate that this drive has really suffered such terrible damage? On the contrary, is it not at least plausible that the repression leading to neurosis is caused by the repressing of other, usually considered higher, instincts? Have the religious and moral instincts—or, if we do not like to call them "instincts," those factual, inherited or acquired religious and moral forces, emotions, imaginings, needs—been treated more mercifully by contemporary ruling powers than the lower instincts have? May it not be that these *higher* instincts, needs, and forces, the religious and moral, have suffered damage, and that repression and neuroses have their bases just in this?

At this point an interesting perspective presents itself. From this perspective the psychoanalyst's language about repression takes on real meaning, even from a Christian point of view. Without denying that repression can take place even in the order usually insisted on by psychoanalysis, one may certainly with good reason question whether or not the order between repressive and repressed forces may not be diametrically opposite to each other, and if, so to say, the finest kind of nervousness and the most dangerous center of unrest do not come about through repression of just this kind. Is it not conceivable that the subdued murmur which emerges from the innermost recesses of the souls of men, distorted in every manner, and which in our day especially expresses itself in the much publicized general nervousness and anxiety, finally, however muffled, becomes the threatening language of the inclosed, forgotten and suppressed religio-moral needs? Were one to grant the uneasiness of heart, which cannot find rest except in God, a primordial right to native status among the soul's endowments similar to the one granted to the drives of the "life stream," then one must unconditionally and of necessity deal with this question.

If at one and the same time one is to speak about the tremendous spread of nervousness in this day and to seek causes for neuroses in suppressed contents of the mind, it would perhaps lie closest at hand to consider the prohibition with which the spirit of the times and the whole outlook of the day has clothed the religio-moral senses, and not to concentrate on the comparatively weak drag which the same spirit of the times and the outlook have placed on the libido and on the instincts and drives which we are accustomed to consider as of the *lower* order in human life.

Indeed, it is also admitted by certain trends in psychoanalysis that there is the possibility of another order in repression according to which not the lower but the higher life in man is repressed. Such an admission is made, for example, by Em. af Geijerstam of Gothenburg: "Even the religious sense may, by means of repression, be relegated to the unconscious."[9] Neurosis could accordingly have its basis also in this that the religious sense has been enclosed in the unconscious, and that its emotional energy with bewildered expression now seeks to force its way through the barriers to the conscious.

This sounds quite appealing, but it is of little significance. Because, what is this religious sense of which is spoken? In reality it is *one*, that is, inseparably connected, with the outflowing life energy itself. One may call it libido or anything else. "There is something inside of man which must come out." "It is an interest, a longing which wants to be satisfied."[10] That is all there is to it. There is nothing new or remarkable in the concession that even the religious sense may become an object for repression, when the religious sense is identified with the libido!

It seems to me the author comes closer to the position I have maintained in terms of my understanding of the order between the forces involved in repression when he says that the essence of the problem of neurosis is ethical in character, and that the conquering of the neurosis is an ethical assignment. He implies that that which has been forced back in the neurosis is also an ethical force: the craving for activity, desire for work, unselfish devotion. The nervous person is an egoist. Liberate him from his nervousness and his egoism will give way, and his sense of duty and desire for work will return. This is undoubtedly correct and extraordinarily interesting. But one becomes immediately wary of the idea or the proposed road to liberation, when one is given to understand that the desire for work is in itself an outlet for the general life energy, and is at last at one with the general ecstatic self-dedication, which especially manifests itself in sexual potency. That it nevertheless can be said

44

that there is a correct trend behind the words of Geijerstam I shall show later. However, as long as one places everything of positive value, all items of intrinsic merit for life and its enrichment, in the monistically regarded life stream alone and critically eliminates from ethical values both law and duty, which from time to time resist spontaneous life energy, there is no possibility of escaping the vicious circle. The circle can be broken only when the ethical demand is not only acknowledged but is made into a criterion for a proper distinction between different qualities in the outflowing life energy or life devotion. It is obvious that Geijerstam is quite willing to come to the aid of morality by means of the liberation of this rapturous ecstacy. Of this there can be no doubt. But not all devotion of this sort is ethical, whether it be sexual desire or zest for activity. The specific significance of morality is obviously this, that it shall constitute the enriching element and regulatory force for life's ecstatic devotion, without being legalistic and repressive. I shall presently return to this matter.

With this I have touched upon the first objection to psychoanalytical doctrines regarding repression and neurosis. I have asked if the direction and order between the repressing and the repressed forces is not something other than that presupposed by psychoanalysis: if it is not religious and moral forces in man that are *repressed* instead of being

45

the repressing forces, if it is not the "child within," the better self, which has been silenced and cut off from connection with conscious life, if it is not conscience and the moral forces which have become "constricted" and now send bewildered, obscure, threatening, or wistful voices into the conscious life.

But this objection in reality only involves the step to another objection. And on this second objection, according to my conception of the matter, falls the whole emphasis. That a repression occurs does not in the final analysis depend on the fact that the one drive or force has been too weak and the other too strong, but rather on this, that both have had the balance of power, in the sense that both have been equally strong or equally weak. This is absolutely decisive in the whole process of repression. Repression and the concentration of neuroses in the deepest levels of the mind do not come into being because the moral force which has encountered the unpermitted desire has been too strong, but rather because it has been too weak! It has not been strong enough to dominate the *drive*. The whole mechanism of repression depends on this fundamental condition. The fact is, it becomes *repression* and not *domination* when the drive which demands to come to the fore is too weak to do so, and the force that would restrain it likewise is too weak really to overpower the drive. Repression is, then, in general a phenomenon of weakness and general helplessness.

Consequently, it is not the moral authority that wins the day, when it restrains drives and emotions, and constricts them. Morality in this situation is too weak to win and too strong to let the drive win: the conflict is not resolved, it is merely postponed. On this account, the developed psychic state is a mixture of a bad conscience and an unsatisfied drive.

Since psychoanalysis itself ascertains that a sense of guilt enters the repressed unconscious, it thereby affirms the accuracy of this conclusion. It simply ascribes to morality a role so powerful as to bring about this psychic condition and with little reason complains about its encroachment in the same manner as it considers the emergence of the sense of guilt and the need for expiation in neuroses as something pathological or at least needless, which the person in question could have been spared. The presupposition for this way of looking at things is, as already stated, the conviction regarding the unnecessarily powerful censure on the part of morality. As a matter of fact, the very content of the repressed testifies to the contrary: morality has shown itself to be entirely too weak to cope with the demands of the drive.

In *one* area one may quite clearly see that a *relaxing* morality involves a very serious danger of neurosis. Much has been said regarding the sexual difficulties among the young people, or more accurately, in reference to youth that has grown to maturity without the opportunity for marriage due to the economic organization of the present social order, where in one's earlier years it is difficult to earn a livelihood sufficient to set up a home and rear a family. It is supposed that neurosis has come into being because of this sexual need. Of course, a causal factor may be found in this postponement of marriage. But it does not explain everything. The nervousness due to restraint upon the sex drive has its basis largely in the fact that the moral consciousness which says, "It is obvious that one must not give way to the sexual drive before marriage," has been shaken; its authority has lost validity. And that which—among other things and more than much else—has shaken this authority has been the physician's earlier insistence that continence is dangerous to health. (To be sure, the situation has changed to a great extent.) Anyway, when the authority of the physician has been set up over against moral authority, the *drive* has as a matter of course lined up with the physician. Quite naturally, and in conjunction with this, we have our modern general philosophy of life with its disintegrating effect in reference to morality and religion. This outlook on life is also known to say: "To do so and so is quite all right," and when year after year and decade after decade this is dinned into the ears, it will take a moral authority of tremendous strength to hold its ground.

Now that authority in this area has been shaken and undermined, what are the consequences? In the first place, the obvious result is loose living and libertinism. But not only this. With many it has not gone this far nor led to this result; the process of undermining has ceased halfway. They remain in a state of uncertainty as to whether or not "it is proper." Their moral consciousness has held them back, but on the other hand, they have been unable to keep from listening to the modern champions of the right to a free exercise of the drive, or to the physician's assurance that this natural course of action is sound. Simply this fact, that there has been a shaking of the obvious necessity to abstain has been fateful, fateful for the very persons who have a stronger moral sense. In such cases it has frequently led not to libertinism, but to nervousness.

Whence has the nervousness come in cases of this sort? Certainly not because, in the first place, the sex drive has been hindered from running its course, but rather because faith and personal conviction that it is necessary to abstain have been shaken. If the suspicion that moral law in this matter makes unreasonable demands had never arisen, the neurosis-generating conflict would never have come about.

The psychical law here involved may be studied in young people coming from different homes with moral authorities of varying strength in their rearing. Not only in reference to sexual life, but in all other areas of life, it may be validly asserted that he who through the support of a strong moral authority has become used to consider it a completely self-evident matter that "it will not do" for him as long as he remains steadfast is it immeasurably more easy to resist temptation; indeed, he will largely be liberated from the temptation itself. He who carries with him from home the holy necessity of a strong moral authority has in this a defense against the special defect of our day, nervousness.

The cure for "the sexual distress" for the present is, therefore, not simply a reform of society, which reform would make earlier marriage possible, or bring about a change in the general moral concept of sexuality, but to bring about rather steadfast conviction that in and of itself it is necessary to refrain from satisfying the drive except under legitimate conditions. If this faith and certainty becomes firm and well established, it will at the same time become a power, a spontaneously working power, which will constitute a most effective bulwark against both libertinism and nervousness. Moral authority and power become a source of neurosis only when they have lost some of their force, when they have lost inherent clarity and necessity and have begun to totter.

Herewith I have in fact already assumed opposition to the present-day diagnosis and derivation of the generally widespread nervousness insisted on by psychoanalysis. The basis for it is not to be found in any powerful encroachment on the part of morality; rather it is to be located in its status of ineffectiveness. For is not this the characteristic of our situation: a people who have lost spiritual attachment to an undoubted, uncontradictable moral authority, under whose power one might have defied the natural impulses? In the final analysis, man of today is especially plagued because he suffers the lack of authority, an authority which should have been powerful enough to force him in his innermost being with the power of an overwhelming, inescapable *necessity* in his moral training, and with the power of an overwhelming, captivating, and saving supernatural power. The authority is so weak that it merely produces "repression." It is not a law that rules. Law has become "legalistic," and legalism is a weakness in "the law," or a weakness in the authority, a weakness fraught with great danger to mental health. If one is to talk about nervousness and anxiety as a general mental ailment, one must seek the ultimate cause, at this point, in this lack of a sound, indisputable moral authority—but *at the same time* it must surely be sought in the lack of a sound, liberating, *religious* authority. I shall return to this later.

The higher moral forces in man have been set free from any binding authority. They have lost their moorings and are adrift. They have become uncertain as to their function. They have not known if they should any longer keep the floodgates closed to the impulse drives of the lower instincts, the instinct of self-preservation, the instinct of domination, the sex instinct, etc. The man of today is not convinced as to anything *necessary* in these matters. He has hesitated as to whether he should let these instincts loose, or he *has* let them loose—to some extent. But he has again become hesitant and undecided. Moral tradition and training, mores and law, have acted as a check, authority has continued active, even where one thought himself essentially set free from it. The lower, disintegrating forces have thus been restrained again. They had been given the *promise* to express themselves; the modern philosophy of life, the wilted Christian authority, everything that once was held as of supernatural obligation, but which is no longer valid—all of this promised liberty. In the course of time, however, because of every sort of conscious and unconscious consideration, it has been impossible to keep the promise. This give and take, which characterizes a situation without authority, has generated a state of insecurity, a tremor in the souls of men which is definitely in every case a very active factor in the modern general nervousness and anxiety.

For this reason, the sense of guilt and the bad conscience are a potently integrating factor in this nervousness. A bad conscience trails along in so far as a person in thought, feeling, or will has given license without a corresponding conviction of right therein. Psychoanalysis is undoubtedly in the right when it points out that this process develops largely in the unconscious. For this reason it is easily concealed from the victim of neurosis that the deepest anxiety lies hidden in the guilt. In spite of this it blazes forth at every point in the nervous life of the man in the street. It evidences itself in the troubled restlessness which pursues him and in the warped sense of duty which governs him. He senses his disobedience to the inciting law which continually demands renewed effort and increased activity as a sort of subdued claim of guilt. He cannot be still without having a "bad conscience." It is to play false to one's duty, even if one spends a little too much time in devotional quietude, in prayer, and contemplation. "Duty" does not allow him to settle himself into anything like Spinoza's "sub specie aeternitatis" where for a moment he might be permitted to remove himself from the everyday stream of life, and gather to himself spiritual renewal, a purer vision of life, and a better sense of values. "Duty" hinders him from religious absorption and fellowship with God!

Contemporary man is definitely unacquainted with the sense of guilt. But this sense makes its appearance in strange forms and associations. It seems to be something one would not bring to the pastor. Moreover, it never really presents itself in the daylight of the conscious.

Why does man clothe his repugnance with emotions which, in spite of this disguise, move in the direction of the experience of a bad conscience and of guilt? The reply could be: It is the unconscious aftereffect of an earlier, entrenched, "forgotten" moral censure. This repugnance and nervousness or guilt feeling, coming forth in new manifestations, constitute the punishment the person suffering from repression has the need to place upon himself [11] It is quite possible that this is the way it behaves. Moreover, must one not also add that here is uncovered fundamental human nature in disfigured form? The reaction associated with this sense of guilt and the need of punishment is a sound one, but its manifestation in warped forms of nervousness and a harassing sense of duty evidence a guilt consciousness that is adrift, or gone astray, which is so much the worse because it has no one in whose presence it may feel this guilt, or to whom an accounting for one's deeds may be made. Is not this

54

that which characterizes our situation: Man as such cannot do anything but heap guilt upon himself in all his ways, but the man of today does not feel that he has anyone to whom he may go with his guilt, one who ultimately places him against the wall with all his guilt, but who also liberates him from it; no one who allows him a forum where he can be tried and judged, where a crisis can be reached and a decision rendered? Is it not this that constitutes the modern mental distress, in so far as one may speak of it in general terms, that man really cannot make clear to himself the nature of his guilt and experience it as such, because he has not apprehended any spiritual force so clearly in his outlook as to make it impossible for this guilt consciousness to arise for him? In the case of Luther's spiritual distress it worked rather nicely. As to its content, his distress was quite definitely established as a guilty conscience, wherein was also included his pathological agony of soul. But the situation is considerably worse today with reference to the muffled anxiety at the very bottom of men's souls, an anxiety that is unconscious of its basis and content. It is this unclarified spiritual need which has made *our* life "under the law" so much more dreadful as it activates emotions without a goal. "The actions" to which it drives have no God before whom to pause, before whom to reflect, before whom to deepen oneself, but have only the tendency endlessly to lengthen the road, increase the tempo of activity, and promote superficiality still further.

Contemporary man conceals unconscious guilt. But an unresolved guilt conflict in the soul does not disappear simply by being forgotten. Neither does it allow itself to be without some evidence. It may be covered up and hidden; it may sink to the level of the subconscious. At times it may emerge in the conscious and spread itself in the mind with its strange, troubling, enervating power and betray the role it is playing under the surface of the conscious. It may also sink so deeply that it can never again rise to consciousness. But it is not therefore ineffective. In a thousand ways it finds opportunities to influence our inner life and overt actions. How much of the atmosphere of mental peace or anxiety we now possess depends on what we consciously do, how many of our decisions and deeds are a result of our conscious deliberations. Let one guilt conflict after another be buried in forgetfulness: they will all rise from the tomb, when their hour is come, and they will be haunting us like ghosts in our emotions, thoughts, wills, and deeds.

It is, therefore, the most dreadful lack of mercy one can show a person not to give him the opportunity to unburden himself of his guilt, or like the proud stoic coldly refuse to admit that an injustice has been done to one, not to seek "revenge" in any way, to shut out the possibilities for reconciliation for the release of the poisoning, negative emotions harbored by the wrongdoer. A worse kind of unmercifulness—rather it is the same case in a different form—is not to let a person see that it *is* guilt, not to let him become conscious of the real implications of the conflict, but let him sway to and fro in uncertainty as the forces of powerlessness and disquietude that rage within him. This is actually what is happening to people today. It is a dreadful agony—or should we say punishment?—that thus has to be endured. The moral disobedience has led to a point where the moral agency in the man is itself unreliable in its reaction, where that which really should be recognized as guilt, is experienced as a general sense of anguish, which by its own indefiniteness makes the road to liberation more difficult.

From this it is evident that my intention is that the diagnosis which in this manner may be made from a Christian and ethical point of view and applied to present-day mental "ailment," may actually employ the methodology of psychoanalysis. The psychoanalytical doctrine of repression is of real aid to a better insight into what occurs in the workshop of the inner life, in the battle between the two powers betwixt which the life of man is placed. Only this must be considered, however: here one takes account of a different order and a different relative position of the forces involved in the process of repression from those ordinarily presupposed by psychoanalysis. Above everything else every semblance must be removed of the concept that the neurosis is due to the granting of too large an area of influence to the religious and moral forces. The fault has *not* been that the moral force has been too strong, so that it has not permitted the drift life to exercise its rightful function; rather the fault is that it has been too weak. It has been so weak that it has not been able to stop the lower drift life from taking the lead; but it has, however, been sufficiently strong, and just as a repressed force sufficiently strong, to hinder the drive from working itself out with a good conscience or retain a mental balance. In this manner, then, has this status of weakness come about, which on the surface appears as nervousness but which at its depth is guilt.

NOTES AND REFERENCES

[1] *Analytische Seelsorge*, p. 13.
[2] *Ibid*, p. 137.
[3] *Korset och livsbägaren*, p. 97.
[4] Franz Alexander: *Psychoanalyse der Gesamtpersönlichkeit*, pp. 24 ff.
[5] *Analytische Seelsorge*, p. 56 (Italics by the author).
[6] Cf. Pfister: *Op. Cit.*, p. 144 "In the newer pedagogical science there is above all else a concept of duty, built on repression and despising love, which has eaten away at the roots of personality and destroyed the most glorious creative powers."
Cf. also Pfister: *Die Psychoanalytische Methode*, p. 567.
[7] Cf. Maeder: *Psychoanalyse und Synthese, Arzt u. Seelsorger*, Vol. 8, p. 20.
[8] Freud: *Ges. Schr.*, Vol. VII, p. 332.
[9] *Medicinsk revue*, 1922, p. 114.
[10] *Ibid..* p. 120.
[11] Cf. Fr. Alexander: *Psychoanalyse der Gesamtpersönlichkeit*, p. 49.

IV

NERVOUSNESS AND INHIBITED
SELF-SURRENDER

ONE MAY STUDY the spiritual side of man's life through history from the point of view of tension between two spiritual forces. The tension becomes most clearly visible and strongly perceivable within Christian history; but it is not limited to the Christian arena. This tension is between law and demand on the one side and grace and love on the other—between a morally demanding force and a religiously liberating force. At different times one or the other has been pushed into the foreground. That one of the forces has been pushed into the foreground and has crowded the other back has always been an indication of weakness and a symptom of the fact that both have suffered. They must always suffer if they are not kept together in unity. "The law" is never strong enough if it is separated from love and grace; and grace and love are never rich and deep enough if they are separated from law and demand, particularly if they are set forth at the expense of the latter. This may be seen in Christianity before Luther. It is difficult to state whether the medieval concept's greatest fault was that it made the law too strict and difficult or too easily kept; if it made the gospel with its love too inaccessible or its accessibility too easy. In reality it did both. Medieval Christianity was *legalistic;* but this means that it lowered the demand to the point where it became possible for man to meet it. It was not so strict as to close every avenue but the narrow path of faith. It gave easy access to grace in so far as it was possible by one's own deeds to acquire it. But it made accessibility difficult in so far as it was not by grace alone that it could be gained, but also by one's own deeds.

Luther made it both easier and more difficult to become and remain a Christian. Comparatively speaking, the accent is on the increased difficulty. This is easily forgotten when one thinks of Luther's work of liberation. He stepped up the demands of the law to a point quite beyond the reach of man. Right here, in Luther's increased demands upon himself, the Reformation has its root. Simultaneously, however, he fought Roman legalistic Christianity which excluded the Christian from a good conscience and assurance of salvation because it taught the comfortless and endless way to salvation by means of one's own deeds. He made it more difficult to appropriate the Gospel—God's grace. It could not be bought with one's own deeds or with indulgence money; it could not be portioned out.

One had God, or one had nothing. But he made it easier in the sense that the grace of God was already an accessible reality by way of faith without these deeds. Easier? As if faith were a simple matter! It was *easy,* since God did it all; but it was more difficult and more painful than all the performances. Faith was really the *faith of forgiveness:* it was a matter of receiving mercy. And for man there is nothing so difficult as to live on pure mercy. This means that God's love is to be found in exactly the same place where the demand of law is stepped up to its highest. Salvation from distress lies at the point where an infinitely increased demand intersects infinite love. That is, salvation lies in the fusion of a *personal unity of law and love.*

In this tension-filled history and alternating fight between law and grace, the theory and practice of psychoanalysis may be applied. It will then be possible better to observe what there is in it that arouses our sympathy, but also our apprehensions.

In every case there is one thing quite characteristic of psychoanalysis: it does not make the law difficult. In the law, in the moral demand, it beholds an enemy as surely as the law suppresses powers of self-surrender in man, the free development of which is a condition for free growth of life. This is, then, the basic tendency in psychoanalysis: to make "grace" or love more easily accessible, and to let its fountains flow without conditions too restraining—

although what kind of "grace" and "love" is intended, is quite another matter.

One must not overlook the force and justice psychoanalysis has in this position. But first and foremost, one must understand that the ecstasy with which this gospel message is received is a symptom of a condition over which we reflect only too little: the symptom which indicates we have lived and are living under a legalistic pressure, a pressure which has made it difficult for us to come in contact with the springs of strength associated with the religious life.

This may occur to some as rather peculiar: that *we* should live under legal pressure—we, emancipated people of this present age! This is nevertheless the case. I have already presented one of the reasons for this. *One always comes under legal pressure when authority is relaxed, when the stern profundity of demand, when necessity and personally clear conviction, diminishes, and there is bargaining as to the possibility of an exemption.* One comes under the pressure of law when the self-evident absolutism of law ceases! It is in such a position we now find ourselves. It is the real, deep-going cause for the present neurosis or, more exactly, *one* of the causes. Contemporary man does not have in his possession any moral authority, which with overwhelming force and without reflective doubt grips his inner life. Moral authority wavers; and when this happens, conditions enter in which especially lend themselves to "repression"; this is a postponing compromise with moral conflict and for the benefit of a pathological sense of guilt or neuroticism. All this, because the sense of guilt can remain healthy only in the face of a law which is strict and insensitive to pleading; a law which can be fulfilled only in a superhuman compassionate love and which is at *one* with this love.

"Law" has become "legalistic." Psychoanalysis as such is a very serious symptom of this legalism, or more correctly, of the effort to escape from it. It has sensed and seen the pressure of legalism and has desired to give aid in the removal of the same. And in so far as we ourselves feel this distress, it is for us to appreciate the value and propriety of its intentions.

In the previous chapter I sought, with the aid of the methodology of psychoanalysis itself, to come to terms with the problem of neurosis and guilt as a history of repression. Viewed according to its content, however, my whole presentation went contrary to the main outline of psychoanalysis. In more direct terms, this contradiction would take this form: If psychoanalysis would view the real ground for repression and neurosis in too severe morality, or in the moral barrier restraining the life stream, I would instead see the deepest basis for this in an insufficiently steadfast moral authority, which from the start could prune the unpermissible releases of the drive, without repressing it to the unconscious. I also mean to imply that it is necessary to speak on behalf of morality against the loose tendencies within psychoanalysis.

But the matter also has another side. This concerns not only morality, but religion also. It is not simply a matter of letting the spiritual force, which represents the demand, come into its own, but a similar force, representing love must likewise come into its own. It is necessary to leave room for the gospel, for grace, because if they fall short, all is lost; the firm moral authority itself would then remain only an idea without anchorage in reality.

On the whole this is what I should like to emphasize: the cause for the spiritual defect of our day, and for that matter, for the religio-moral conflicts grounded in neurosis, is ultimately not to be found only in the lack of a powerful moral authority. It may be found at the same time, in the dearth of a strong religious authority. That is to say, the nervous man, or the person with dual tendencies because of moral demands and the buffeting of insistent drives, has not found any authority to which he may cling and into the arms of which he may throw himself without reservation, something he may love and believe; not necessarily an obligating authority to which to submit, but also no releasing authority to which to attach himself! At this juncture it is possible, in all seriousness to unite with the principal tenet of psychoanalysis. Psychoanalysis has really had a genuine sense or insight that the basic cause of neurosis guilt lies in that "the spontaneous life instinct" has not been allowed to live itself out, that is, restraining forces have caught and enchained it. Were we to express this in old-fashioned religious language, it would take this form: psychoanalysis has seen that man, above all, needs *freedom from the law*. Freedom from the law? Have I not just said that it is the absence of a strong and imperatively overmastering law that causes nervousness? And even so, there appears to be no objection up to this point. Man of today suffers under a law which has the effect of being "legalistic." He suffers under a law which hinders him from giving expression to the drive of self-surrender. In many forms this law may feel at home in natural law as well as in moral law. But finally it is always the same force which jealously closes that door in man through which the self-sacrificing powers would seek their way out.

It ultimately comes to this—it is the need for self-surrender, the life-sacrificing drive,[1] and love that have been enclosed and repressed. In this psychoanalysis is quite right. In so far as with such words as libido, eros, etc., it merely wishes to state that fervent devotion is the profoundest vital force in man, it is quite right also from a Christian point of view. The inability of the nervous person to attain a spontaneous, naive joy of life is evidence of this hemmed in or frustrated need for devotedness. Moreover, man's moral deficiency, his unpleasant harassing sense of duty, his sense of ennui in his work, have their roots in the confinement of the urge for fervent devotion that is within him.

Ennui in reference to work? Contemporary man may or may not be neurotic, but is it not without rhyme or reason to accuse him of this? If anyone works, surely it is the man of today, that is, if he can get work. Rather, is not the danger that he works too hard and should be held back? Truly, is it not overexertion that brings about neuroticism? Anagogical psychoanalysis is surely quite right when it answers this question with an emphatic *no*. It is not overexertion that causes neuroticism; it is the tedium connected with the tempo of life, attending to one's duty, the effort to assume one's assignments—with which one must nevertheless eventually but reluctantly deal. He who with life, enthusiasm, interest, and joy in his calling dedicates himself to his work does not become tired or nervous. As an antidote let the inner resources of devotion, enthusiasm for life and labor, issue forth, unhindered by legalistic barriers which have been set up by pseudo-evangelical Christianity or human prejudice.

Enthusiasm for work and life will come, if you

succeed in overcoming nervousness, if you succeed in conquering the restraining ethical conflict and sense of guilt. This is the position taken by psychoanalysis, and this is also the position taken by Christianity. The latter may state the case in similar words: neuroticism suffers from a lack of religious devotion and faith. There the whole fault lies. Psychoanalysts can say the same thing.[2] With the devotion that is of faith one achieves the joy and enthusiasm of life related to one's calling. With religious faith come the moral life and the good deeds as fruit on a good tree. This concomitance reaches even further. This new faith and enthusiasm cannot be produced through one's own wisdom and power. "Our interest in work is conditioned by factors quite different from our own will. This is bestowed upon us as grace from the depth of our own being, and our ego must remain in contact with this depth, in order that we may be in a position to labor with vigor and enthusiasm," writes Iwan Bratt.[3]

At this juncture, psychoanalysis appears to have the proper insight as judged from a Christian point of view; that which causes suffering in the neurotic with his hidden sense of guilt, and suffering in the nervous man in general, is the lack of devotedness. He cannot experience a spontaneous, naive joy of life; he cannot attack his assignments with brisk courage and a sound will; he cannot meet death with an unflinching eye, because the channel for ecstatic devotion within him has been closed. This also has been recognized by psychoanalysis.[4]

Even more interesting perhaps is what from the anagogical side of psychoanalysis especially is said in answer to the accusation against psychoanalysis to the effect that it lacks moral seriousness. Is it not an undermining of morality to make the moral forces, in comparison with all others, the one repressing and neurosis producing factor, to make of *conscience* a creator of a spiritual pathological center? Geijerstam and Bratt reply: The *negative* conscience is not the most important authority for morality; rather, it is the positive conscience. And the positive conscience, the highest moral demand, is that the devotedness within man be given free course.

From a strictly formal view, this comes very close to evangelical ethics. Obviously this is very much the same as Luther's intention when he says that the first commandment in the Decalog is the most important of all, which simply demands man's surrender to faith. The commandment about the setting free of the drive of devotedness is the supreme measure of morality. Geijerstam may also, with a certain amount of justice, call on Luther when he, in the face of this demand, takes the concept of conscience into consideration. Because, for Luther also, conscience has in its loftiest meaning a religious, positive function: "Conscience is that organ in man which has to deal with his purely religious state; that organ with which the grace of God is received by him through faith."[5]

And yet here, where these differing points of view formally approach each other the closest, they find themselves factually quite far apart. Because the question is: *When* really does this positive conscience function? In other words: What is the right kind of devotedness? What is the criterion whereby it can be judged that it is the conscience which is functioning and not simply a general drive of devotedness that exerts pressure? For with Luther it is not insisting on any indefinite devotion when he talks about the devotedness of faith and the higher claims of conscience. It is rather a devotion of a particular kind with its own special criterion; and it is just *because* of this that he can use the concept of conscience in reference to the satisfying of this drive.

It is obvious that we are now at the parting of the ways so far as Christianity and psychoanalysis are concerned. The channel for man's devotion must be opened. In this psychoanalysis is quite right. It is also quite right in claiming that this channel is closed for modern man because he is ensnared in legalism. But Christianity adds: Man's devotion to the assignments of life is restrained; he cannot with courage and caution encounter life and death. This is due to the fact that in some measure the deepest channels of devotedness within him are closed, and therefore the profoundest devotion is arrested. Because of this, disturbances are set up on all levels of life and a chase is started on the surface levels of life, to find substitutes for the failing joy and devotedness deep within. The letting loose of the lower drives are part and parcel of these substitutes. The one who at the center of his life is restless desires to benumb his disturbance, and somehow satisfy his empty heart. He surely will not be sparing with his "life energy." He will expend himself in a dizzy squander or the hurry-scurry of work. He will probably redouble the tempo of life in order to escape from the uneasiness of his innermost being. Here we find an increased development of energy together with heartfelt aversion; an increased tempo of work with an inner sense of tedium with work. Whence should a person in this situation gather his spontaneous, naive enjoyment and uncalculated joy in life? His entire interest is taken up by the effort to substitute for the *lack* of a more profound joy.

The deepest channel of ecstatic devotion must be opened. The question is, which is it? Psychoanalysis readily replies: It is the sex drive. Ultimately this means the same, whether it is interpreted more as something mental, or is taken literally. Enthusiasm in one's work, the joy of life, etc., all taken together are really in the final analysis one with the healthy pulsating sex drive, or evidence of its vitality. In any case, it—namely, the sex drive—cannot by any criterion be differentiated from the general devotion drive, eros, or libido. "We have," says Geijerstam,[6] "in our present position no sure criterion when we attempt to judge whether or not a given expression of energy is sexual." This observation is demonstrated further in "anagogical" psychoanalysis, relatively free from Freud, where it is noted that the configurating symbols in dreams, from one field or another, may act as substitutes, the one for the other. Sexual dream images relate something about the dreamer's attitude to his work and other duties. Ennui in one's work and neurosis-forming escapism from one's obligations are signs of sexual impotence, or an expression thereof. If one recovers from this ennui, that in itself is a sign that the sex drive is pulsating in a healthy manner. This does not suggest that the prescription for the nervous person who suffers from disinclination to work is simply to seek out the opposite sex. Obviously this would not relieve the repressed psychic complex which constitutes the seat of neurosis. This complex must be set free, or rather, it must be attached to the conscious. Only in this way can devotion relative to the sex drive have a wholesome expression. A person who formerly was neurotic can be considered recovered and sound when he is

71

sexually vigorous, which is evidence that the process of soul cure has been successful. This appears also to be the position taken by the rather independent anagogical school, as over against Freud.

It is not surprising that this drive, the sex drive, is looked upon with the deepest reverence. It is God in us, says Dr. Strömme of Oslo, in his book, *Nervositet*.[7] The slumbering sex drive in the unconscious represents the progressive affirmation of life within us. According to Strömme, who has adopted the religious terminology, it may at the same time be the religious faith and love; and the object: the God to which faith may attach itself. Religious faith is excellent, says Strömme, and Christian faith is best of all; but no objective counterpart for the devotion of faith is necessary. A subjective god is quite sufficient, which is to say: one's own devotion drive, faith in one's own faith, is sufficient. The human libido has taken the place of divine love, and must serve at once both as subject and object of the religious situation. "Faith" and "conversion" are terms used in this connection; or else an equally nice word is used, "transformation of personality."[8] But how shall this transformation come about? Is it done in this manner: By faith one accepts and clings to one's own devotedness, now released by analysis, or by attachment to an other-than-human object, an ideal? We shall soon return to this question.

72

The great teacher at the fountainhead of psycho-analysis would definitely disagree with this religious proclamation.[9] But as a matter of fact, it is a logical offshoot from the basic theory. Where the vital value of the unrestrained drive is so strongly accentuated, as is factually the case in Freud's psychology, there is but a step to its actual idolization. A religion on this basis can ultimately not become anything but man's self-loving communion with himself. The theory about "the life stream" never permits him to arrive at a human level. The love which is to rescue and save us, or at least make us "well" and "normal," if it is allowed to spring forth unrestrained or sublimated, is not a superhuman love which takes hold of us and to which we can flee *away from* ourselves without any human resources.

The psychoanalytical doctrine and practice of release, which we shall now examine more closely, show traces of a real struggle with the problem which hereby is intimated.

NOTES AND REFERENCES

[1] When in these writings I speak about self-surrender (literally, "the drive of ecstatic devotion"), or something similar, as a constitutive part of man; and when under this heading I include, for purposes of comparison, the libido of psychoanalysis, the sense of fellowship and self-sacrifice found in individual psychology, as well as the devotional love and faith of Christianity, I am naturally fully aware of the differentia involved in the various concepts. At first glance, the inclusion of so many seemingly varied concepts may appear like a sweeping generalization. However, there is something generic about it, no matter how varied the connotations

may be. The several schools of thought have one denotative thing in mind: they concentrate on a structural reality in man, which in its necessity and spontaneity drives towards a similar goal—a way out from the shackles of legalism, from selfishness, from the strains of living up to the banalities of life. It is a matter of freedom in a direction that seems instinctively right regardless of price. These remarks appear to be necessitated by the charge from some of my critics who have seemingly misunderstood my point of view, thinking as they seem to do, that I have employed "libido" and "agape" indiscriminately.

[2] Geijerstam: *Fortschritte der Sexualwissenschaft und Psychoanalyse*, Vol. I., p. 387.

[3] *Splittring och enhet*, p. 100. Cf. Poul Bjerre: *Korset och livsbägaren*, p. 106: "We are forced to the admission that what a person does is not of the greatest importance; with all respect due his actions and passions, *what really happens to him* is more important than anything else."

[4] Geijerstam: *Medicinsk revue*, 1922, p. 132. And, *Zur Frage des Verdrängungsproblems. Acta psychiatrica et neurologica*, Vol. II, Fasc. 1, 1927, p. 35.

[5] Arvid Runestam: *Den kristliga friheten hos Luther och Melanchton*, p. 162.

[6] *Medical Review*, 1922, p. 117. Note 2.

[7] *Ibid.*, p. 288.

[8] I. Bratt: *Splittring och enhet*, p. 101 ff.

[9] See his criticism of religion in *Die Zukunft einer Illusion*, 1927. Also in Swedish.

V

PSYCHOANALYTICAL AND CHRISTIAN DELIVERANCE

THE THEOLOGIZING PSYCHOANALYSIS has found the divine in man's dedication drive itself. Consequently, according to this "theology," man does not need an extra-human God as deliverer. A human technician is quite sufficient—even though this human technician must finally and secretly withdraw as a substitute in the saving process.

Let us see what happens in actual practice when this drive within us breaks forth by the aid of the analyst. How does the psychoanalytical liberation come about? Supposedly, it occurs in this manner: the person suffering from mental or spiritual disturbance, aided by the psychoanalyst, brings the hidden life raging in the unconscious into consciousness.

The psychoanalytic cure, thus presented, involves two basic elements: the one is the matter of raising the repressed complex to the conscious level by special analytical technique. It is essentially an intellectual process. As we have seen, the procedure is as follows: the patient, without pressure on the part of the analyst, freely relates whatever comes to his mind, unfolds his case history, communicates his dreams and other things that may serve as a guide to the analyst in his effort to assist in the discovery of the complex and in attaching it to the conscious. The other element in the analytical deliverance, the "transfer," the personal attachment to the analyst, is essentially emotional. It is not analysis; on the contrary it is synthesis.

Let us dwell for a moment on the first point. As a slogan for its activity, psychoanalysis has adopted the proud Greek expression, "Know thyself." To this it has added two others: "Accept yourself!" and "Be yourself." None of these three expressions need be contrary to Christian thinking. It is quite necessary, even according to the Christian concept, that man shall know himself. This may be brought about by having the light appear more gradually, or it may be a matter of a sudden flash of insight. At times the light must be thrown unmercifully into a person's life, in order that he may be brought into a psychological state in which he shall be able to avail himself of the deliverance. But the question is *when* this light really dawns on him: that is, under what circumstance does he become clear as to what he is and what he should become? Does he really come to this true light by means of psychoanalysis? Does he by this means learn to know himself as he really is? Know himself from every aspect and in all his depths? In good and evil? Granted that certain aspects are revealed, how about the others, which easily flee and hide themselves from the view of the analyst? Do these aspects come into focus in this self-knowledge?

J. A. Hadfield in his book, *Psychology and Morals* says: "To see ourselves as we really are is an event of profound importance. It is sometimes brought about by the presentation of a new ideal with which we compare ourselves, as in religion. It can also be brought about by analysis. The purpose of all analysis is to discover the whole person, and to reveal a man to himself. This is always a surprise; it is often a shock."[1]

Religion and psychoanalysis accordingly are placed side by side as of equal worth and greatness. The implication is that under one or the other, man may learn to know himself. And through this knowledge of himself, if it be profound enough, salvation and liberation are to be achieved. Self-knowledge can be realized by our being confronted by an ideal in religion. Hadfield, who is kindly disposed toward Christianity, obviously is thinking of the image of Jesus Christ. Before this image we may look at ourselves and analyze ourselves. In doing so we may see what we are. The other way, which Hadfield in reality recommends, is psychoanalysis. And note carefully: here is a human image serving as a "mirror." And it is for the analyst to get the patient to see himself in it. What sort of human image is this which here serves as a mirror for him who would learn to know himself? The answer is: It is a person, conditioned by a free and sublimated development of the libido and sexuality; it is the "natural" man, unsophisticated, possessing basic sensual power and conditioned by sublimated drives. The patient learns to know himself when he is permitted to look down into this workshop of sublimation, where he finds that he himself is actually merely raw material, not good and not evil, but simply physical and psychical raw material. I quote: "Looking down into the depths of one's own soul gives one an insight into what the powers are that govern life, and this insight gives one reverence for these powers. One sees how one's will has been determined by tendencies and influences, from which it follows that one can look more dispassionately on one's own wishes and with a greater ease can give in and say, 'Thy will be done,' if the matter involves a vain desire which disturbs 'the kingdom of heaven' within. Insight into the importance of inner harmony, that it is really 'the one thing needed,' creates an unassuming attitude; thereby one becomes more inclined to be content with one's daily bread. Then one comes to the sense of guilt. One sees how one has been formed by tendencies and environment, and one can with greater ease forgive oneself the folly of one's life, and seek to blot out the past by living in real humble submission to the laws of life. One no longer tortures oneself with remorse but labors to adjust oneself to life."[2]

Now, what is being said here? Put the ethical evaluation of your life out of sight. Look upon yourself and say: This is the way I am, and I can be no different. And should you happen to discover phases of your life unsympathetic with your "ideal self," be not blind, neither judge yourself! Merely put up with the inevitable and adjust yourself.

No Christian will deny that the profound self-knowledge achieved in the presence of Christ is a self-analysis which may bring salvation and liberation. In this Hadfield is quite right. But what does man experience *here;* what kind of self-knowledge does he achieve? It is not merely an indifferent moral raw material that he sees; he also sees sin, evil, and guilt. But there is also something else he sees, and something that appears rather elusive. Foreboding and hope tremble inside; there are hands that reach out and would hold fast to man's image; there is something related to the human ideal that reaches out. There is mourning over neglected possibilities; it is like an abandoned child that cries. But why multiply images? Christianity knows an expressive term for this difficult-to-define, the delicate, tender in man that would escape intrusion. The image of God is what Christianity calls it. It is the image of God in man which is awakened out of its slumber when the most profoundly human and the divine simultaneously affect man. This is the simple psychology of the Bible and Christianity.

What becomes of these shy, timid "forces" in man as he is being mirrored before the human image of psychoanalysis? What becomes of responsibility, sin, and guilt? Does man really learn to know himself? The quivering depth, the foreboding, the self-surrender, the faith, "the child," which reaches for liberty and love, the image of God? Where in psychoanalysis does one find a place for these noble forces in man that give courage and confidence to reach toward liberty and completion? There is no such place. These forces must hide themselves in order not to be sullied. The most profound self-surrender is not realized, and if it were, its existence would be in danger.

A person must "accept himself" states psychoanalysis, with all his drives and propensities, and not shut his eyes to them or drive them away. This might be well and good, if by this it is merely meant that a person shall have the courage to see himself as he really is and acknowledge, without cover up or simulation, his total shabbiness, sin, folly, and wickedness. However, there is also danger in this accepting of one's self such as one appears before the "normal" person presented by psychoanalysis. To accept one's self before this image *may* mean not only honestly to acknowledge and accept the drives which factually govern one, but also to permit drives and appetites to enter into one's life which formerly played no role there. One must not disturb innocence with impure images, even if the images are derived from veritable human nature. It may amount to one's being urged to accept something that actually is not or never has been part of one's being, which came into being the very moment it was called to life—awakened by an image in which one chanced to behold his worse self, one's lower drives reflected. Anyone who has read Freud or Freudian writings has surely not been able to escape sensing something of this danger, even if he has not done so consciously. In the very encounter with the libido-governed human image lies danger of pollution. This encounter could mean dire devaluation of one's self, a slander of the self and the Creator. The picture of this drive-governed man which one meets says: "This is what you are!" And the danger is that one may reply: "Yes, I am just such," and in this reply abandon something delicately noble that one previously possessed.

In this manner psychoanalysis becomes not only poor Christianity, but poor psychology. There is something in the human soul that manages to hide itself from the practicing analyst's technical grasp as well as from the thought forms of analysis. The psychoanalytic methodology is in some ways too coarse to catch the more delicate activities in the human soul.

The human instinct of self-surrender may be awakened and nourished by any number of stimuli. But only *one* such means is adequate for the most profound surrender instinct. It is that stimulus which is so high, pure, and delicate that it is able to vibrate all the invisible, pure, and fine strings which alone can give the song of life its proper melody. In the Christ-image Christianity finds this most adequate stimulus.

Psychoanalysis knows of one substitute for this Savior-image. It is the analyst himself in the transfer. This is the second chief element in the analytical process of liberation. The patient "falls in love" with the analyst. He hovers around him with his thoughts and emotions, raises him to the very sky and regards him as savior—all this, according to reports from the analysts themselves. This indicates, as we have already noted, that it is not the analysis by itself, that is, the clarification of the unconscious for the mind and the consciousness, which is the ultimately decisive in the psychoanalytical deliverance. A new, personal factor has entered in. Somehow a personal prehension is necessary. The surrender does not come about unless it is called to life by a person, to which person it may attach itself. The analyst becomes a deliverer, not merely by aiding in making the unconscious conscious for the

82

mind, not by any intellectual act, not by means of *analysis* alone, but by virtue of his becoming an object for a new personal synthesis in the patient; a synthesis in which the patient collects himself in an emotional outpouring. And now, in the continuation of this synthetic emotion the analyst can at last come to the bottom of things. However, there is also something else of great psychological and Christian interest which supposedly transpires in this transfer and synthesis. According to reports from psychoanalysts, the patient relives his complexes in company with the analyst. He apprehends him with his love, but he also pushes his hatreds, his wickedness, and his negative emotions on him. Whatever presses him, he unloads on the analyst. "It is exactly as if the relation (love and trust) between patient and physician were a line on which they could suspend the symptoms and slide them over to the physician. It is all a device, a fiction, quite analogous to the Christian doctrine of atonement, in that Jesus takes the sins of humanity upon himself, and by His suffering liberates man."[3]

Who can escape noting that the analyst is not satisfied by being merely a technical curer of souls? In a certain measure he enters in as a personal savior. Moreover, at times he reminds us that Jesus was also a psychoanalyst.

This much is now established: By accentuating the role of personal influence in the transfer, one evades the strict intellectualism of the process of liberation; the person is not set free simply because he becomes *conscious* of the evil which broods within him. In addition there must be a personal apprehension.

This manner of viewing the situation, this very "method of salvation" appears quite similar to Christian procedure. It is to be noted that even in Christianity it is a question about both these things: first, the person must be brought to consciousness and clarity as to the true nature of his life, so that he may, without consideration or mercy, peer into the depth of his own life, with the realization that nothing is to be gained by hiding the sensitive spot. But no one is liberated by this clarity or consciousness alone. A personal apprehension is necessary; not mere analysis, but synthesis also.

However, we can hardly escape seeing the difference. In psychoanalysis the two elements, that is, the analysis with the resolving of the complex on the one hand, and the personal surrender on the other, fall apart into quite separate elements. Some rather nice distinctions must be made at this point. To a certain extent, the ingratiating feeling for the analyst intrudes itself as a hindrance in the resolving process itself. The factors involved move along side by side; they do not constitute a single act, however. In other words, it is not the analyst himself who, in his own person and in what he *is*, constitutes the critic and revealer of secrets as he pierces into the depth of the soul. The chief consideration at this point is that sufficiently technical skill and sound procedure, as well as sufficiently sharp psychological insight, detect the malady. The analyst's value as a *person*, or his personal worth, has no role to play in this. To repeat: The chief emphasis seems to be placed on impersonal technical adequacy and skill.

In contrast to this, Christian salvation presents both elements, the loosening of bonds and personal attachment, in one focus. The factor which reveals my inner being is the personal aspect of the same person through whom my faith is awakened and gains a stronghold. This is the case when one encounters the person of *Christ*. It is by virtue of what He *is*, through the "Word" about Him, that clarity is shed over my inner life, and my life is *simultaneously* bound with Him. A personal life meets us in the "Word," which life we cannot escape, if we open ourselves to the essential and realistic history within history. As Bultmann says, one may, if one wishes put "Jesus" in quotation marks as "an abbreviation for the historical phenomenon" here involved: that is, the living personal life which vibrates in the words of the Gospels and which no one spiritually alive can avoid feeling or seeing.[4] In this living Word, then, there is analysis and synthesis for anyone who would expose himself to its power. This is, by the way, the case in the encounter with any profound personality; it is an exposure to critical analysis. But the analytical rigor rests in the same personal value as does the synthetic power. To be sure, analysis may be facilitated by a judicious apprehension on the part of the agent, be he pastor or analyst.

The psychoanalytical treatment, rightly or wrongly, is frequently compared to the Christian confessional. With some finer differentiations, it is at times compared to the Roman Catholic confessional, and then again the comparison tends toward the evangelical idea. Perhaps it has something in common with both points of view. It differs from the Roman in that it patently wants something beyond the confession of, and absolution for, known sins. In agreement with the evangelical view, it is aware that evil is broader and lodges more deeply than it does in particular evil acts. It would reveal the hidden core of the disease and attack evil at its roots. In this it resembles the evangelical confessional. Nevertheless, there is an essential difference, and this difference makes it again similar to the Roman concept, namely its notion of the *impersonal method*. As the analytical technician keeps himself more or less out of sight from the patient, so are the father confessor and the one confessing hidden from each other's sight. In either case, it is soul cure stressing the importance of technique; professional technique on the one hand, and institutional technique on the other. Clearly, neither involves the "technique," if it may be called such, which puts the stress on Christian personality. Here I wish to remark that one must not hastily underestimate the impersonal procedure. Alas! In the evangelical church there has been such an underestimation of the objective institutional and impersonal concept that one hardly is aware of the existence of the institutional confessional. However, the institutional confession, as an institution, will never attain a significance in the evangelical church corresponding to that of the Roman Church, that is, not so long as the former remains evangelical. One must not at this juncture, nor in other areas of religion, expect too much from organizational innovations. It is neither the institution nor the establishment that is primarily at fault. And as far as the confessional in the evangelical church is concerned, it will be in the future as it has been hitherto that personal confidence, by and large, will seek out the person, be he pastor or layman, in whom one may trust. And should this state of affairs change, the necessary consequence would be detrimental to the deeper levels of conscience.

Psychoanalysts are quite right in this that every curer of souls is to a certain extent a deliverer or redeemer. It all depends on *when* he functions as a curer of souls, through which function he delivers, and to what he delivers. If in his own person he applies his redemptive work to man's powers of self-surrender aside from his own religio-ethic personality, he has no right to consider his work as curer of souls, or to compare his function with that of the pastor, the priest, or the confirmation instructor, who truly performs as he should. Surely, the analyst in his role as deliverer should be willing to admit the Christian pastor as an adequate object for comparison. Indeed, this appears to be the case. As one analyst says: "Does one not often see a confirmation instructor become an object of gushing devotion on the part of the confirmands?" True enough! And it is not only the confirmation instructor who easily becomes an object of this gushing adoration. This can happen to the preacher in the pulpit on the part of the audience who are considerably beyond the teen age. But from a Christian point of view this has never been considered normal, nor something that ought to occur; on the contrary, it has been stamped as something morbid, quite out of taste, and at best ridiculous, particularly when this category is made up of the opposite sex. On the part of Christianity, this is condemned mainly as a confusion of eroticism and religion.

On the other hand, psychoanalysts proclaim such "infatuation" as normal, something that ought to be. It is symptomatic of the depth of the liberation desired by Christianity, and the "salvation" aimed at by psychoanalysis. It is not the moral personality of the analyst that "binds" and liberates in the transfer, just as it is not the moral personality in him but rather the technician who is the critically analyzing factor in the liberation of the "suppressed complex" from the unconscious. For this reason, transfer and analysis are matters of considerable risk. This is also emphasized strongly by the more conscientious phychoanalysts. Indeed, it is with good reason that they insist that analysis shall be practiced only by persons of high moral standing. But do they see with equal clarity how potent the temptation is to devote oneself to this source of livelihood without too many scruples where there is so little of control and where the general discernment, if discernment is functioning at all, is so very much less demanding and strict than it is in reference to other soul healers? The risk is quite significant. For who is this person into whose hand helpless man entrusts his life? Is he in a position to undertake the responsibility involved in awakening wellsprings within him which he cannot control? Or does he call into being only such springs as would correspond to his own personal worth, which become simple substitutes and which clip the wings of his aspirations? And when the self-surrender is liberated from the analyst, in what direction does he help the patient to aim? Away from himself to someone stronger? At best this would be the case, if the analyst were a Christian. Otherwise the aim would be in the direction of some suitable mundane assignment, or to a devotional contemplation of his own sense of surrender, contemplation of the god within himself.

Here we find evangelical Christianity interposed between two agencies: the Roman institution with its impersonal mechanics of salvation and impersonal powers of grace, and psychoanalysis with its peculiar mixture of impersonal technique of deliverance and extra-ethical personal integration. In such a position it behooves evangelical Christianity to steer a steady course. Nothing else is worthy of the name salvation, or at least Christian salvation, than that which saves *ethically*. And nothing but personal ethical life can liberate and strengthen the ethical forces in man, at the same time as it breaks down by criticism what is impure and illegitimate (or false). There is no analyst more powerful, more penetrating, with keener sight than a spiritually integrated, forcefully whole personality. He is the more profound analyst, just as at the same time his function is integrating, healing, unifying in his effect on the tattered human soul. "The spiritual maturity which makes a personality fit to lead and help others is not achieved by knowing something, but by being something."[5] And with some justice, the physician, Dr. Herbert Seng, states: "In psychotherapy, he is not the best healer who most thor-

90

oughly analyzes the patient, but he who so vitally formulates certain important problems of the patient that this formulation mediates not only an intellectual apprehension of his situation, but also brings before him insights which otherwise he could behold only under special occasions." And "the higher the ranks of the factors leading to the illness are, the more important for recovery is the therapeutic personality, and less important will be the particular therapeutic acts. It is explainable, then, that it takes a very superior being, one who in himself in a certain measure exemplifies man's spiritual renewal, and consequently man's greatest ideal simply through what he is and aside from any act, to become the powerful impulse which in turn will set in motion the decisive synthesis in the broken, but for reconstruction mature, soul."[6]

The synthesis is actually associated with self-knowledge. Psychoanalysis has never understood the more profound meaning of the Delphic oracle: "Know thyself!" No one learns to know himself in a truly profound sense by a self-reflecting analysis. The longer he continues such an analysis, the more he will discover mere fragments of a disintegrated life. This learning to know oneself in the fullest sense is accomplished in surrendering, self-outpouring, unified emotion. Only he who is renovated in a process of integration knows himself as he emerges from the destructive analysis. And this integration is most profound under the influence of another integrated personality. Such a person becomes at once a profoundly analyzing critic of my life and a restorer of my powers. Ultimately, it is not the analyst who uncovers the depths as he gropes his way into every niche and corner of the human soul. For him the soul would flee and hide. It is rather the person as a whole who so captures a man that he, as it were, forgets to hide, forgets to resist, and yields most humbly. It is this personal synthetic capture of the human soul that precedes the more profound analysis. "It is so impossible for the reflecting mind to maintain order and supervision during periods of depression that it does the opposite and makes the evil sevenfold worse. This confirms the impotence to which man so easily succumbs when he finds himself in solitude and isolation. Should it so happen that in the throngs of historical and living personalities we meet a like-minded person, one who is able to snatch us out of our solitude, everything might all of a sudden be changed. The vitality that flows from this being moves through our soul in a unifying and liberating manner: he has thought out to a final conclusion thoughts after which we have been groping; he has walked the paths we have sought but failed to find; he has beheld the visions we have pursued but which have ever vanished as mirages before our eyes. And above all, he has succeeded in resolving conflicts into which we have run and in which we are held fast, and succeeded in wrestling his way through a world with which we have not been able to come to terms. It is when we yield ourselves to a person whom we acknowledge to be stronger than we are that the miracle of identification takes place. And the greater the surrender is with which we approach the object of our identification, the richer and more complete is the miracle."[7] I have quoted the above at length, finding myself in full agreement, while at the same time, I read and note with consternation how the same author in the same book misunderstands Christian experience, or as in this situation, the "Christ-identification." It is obvious that he is unacquainted with the basic position of evangelical Christianity at this juncture, and particularly its effort to portray Christian experience so that Christ shall not become "a strange intruder in our soul, but rather shall leave its religio-moral autonomy inviolate."

The deliverance, the "analysis," of a human soul must actually aim to lower the resistance to the "psychosynthetical tendency" in the soul. But the psychosynthetical tendency's nature is that it looks for a strong personal life in its encounter with liberation, because it is the yielding of itself to the personal authority which simultaneously heals the broken and opens doors to the secret chambers of the soul.

This has far-reaching consequences for the evaluating of the general practice of psychoanalysis. A forceful, captivating personality may obviate suppression without analytical technique. This does not imply that he eliminates it without the agony of mental surgery, or that he conceals that which ought to be exposed to light. However, it indicates that he exposes to light only what properly ought to be so exposed. And man's generic nature, and the probing into every kind of sensual filth, do not necessarily belong to this category.

Psychoanalysis prides itself on not being easy going in its dealings with mental conflicts. It would not wink at or otherwise obfuscate matters. On the contrary, it desires to stir up things from the very bottom, retrace the concatenation of events, and trace and call attention to the one sensitive spot. In a certain sense, it would remake the past, and provide a new start. In this it appears similar to the Christian *modus operandi* in salvation, and differentiates itself from the salvation methods of Coue and others, who by means of autosuggestion distract attention from evil and deny it. Evil in the soul, as far as psychoanalysis is concerned, is not mere appearance or something imaginary. It is actual, it is real.

But it all depends on *what* depths are being stirred up. Even in this matter the norm for Christianity is the ethical personality. And for all its austerity, this norm is modest. Christianity is not particularly interested in curious meddling with the turbid sensuality of man. It is concerned with deep-seated pathologies of a different sort. But, now about psychoanalysis? What is the object of its probing? It is "the Oedipus complex," sexuality, and that in its earliest stages, before the emergence of conscience and a personality structure. There is no thought of venturing down these lower levels with such an implement as moral remorse. And should one seek and find other depths and later repressions there will be, as we have seen, more explanations in terms of natural causes to throw light on this subject, rather than grave personal condemnation. The great danger of psychoanalysis for the higher spiritual life is undoubtedly this that it considers it necessary to probe into this sullied past in order to remove mental repressions. One may see one's mental illness in terms of the past, one's father and mother complex, one's auto-eroticism and homosexuality and all the rest that the analyst manages to discover in the agitated generic human nature—all done in the naive belief that such a survey will lead to health. It surely cannot be the intention that man shall try to achieve more "consciousness" in his life by acquiring clearer insight through such pursuits. And even if the insight should become clearer, it does not become *purer*.

NOTES AND REFERENCES

[1] J. A. Hadfield, *Psychology and Morals*, R. M. McBride & Co., New York, 1936, pp. 234-5.

[2] I. Bratt: *Splittring och enhet*, p. 109.

[3] Strömme: *Nervösitet*, p. 129.

[4] Rudolf Bultmann, *Jesus*, p. 17.

[5] Tor Andrae: *Psychoanalys och religion*, p. 75.

[6] *Die Heilungen Jesu in medizinischer Beleuchtung*, Arzt u. Seelsorger, Heft 4, p. 16.

[7] Poul Bjerre: *Korset och livsbägaren*, p. 54.

VI

THE IDEAL OF HEALTH AS PRESENTED BY PSYCHOANALYSIS AND CHRISTIANITY

IN ITS DEVELOPMENT another phase of psychoanalysis has come into view. Where psychoanalysis has arrived at some degree of discretion, to the extent of realizing the implications of what has been presented in the foregoing chapter in reference to the Christian doctrine of salvation, it admits of failure in that it has proceeded on false premises. This development has reached a point where it must be admitted that the criticism already presented has been anticipated to some extent among some analysts. However, these developments are resultants which careful analysts would consider quite incidental, and not part and parcel of their practice.

Certainly Pfister would object to any other view. To be sure, he does ascribe great value to psychoanalysis for the Christian cure of souls. But if one were to examine him more closely in his book *Analytische Seelsorge,* one would find that his evaluation of psychoanalysis is such that it is an extension of the assignment of pastoral care. From his presentation one may surmise the following: If the pastor, as the example of Jesus demands, were to extend his compassion to every kind of suffering, he should consequently learn and make use of any and all means suited to each particular aspect of healing. And the fact is that there are ailments which are definitely in need of analytic aid.

This notion establishes a line between cases that may be handled by usual pastoral care, and those that especially lend themselves to analysis. One of the conditions, of course, is that the ailment must involve "repression" in order to indicate the need for analysis. Moreover, the ailing person in this instance should be one of high moral standing.

To this is added an apparently meaningful explanation: psychoanalytical healing does not intend to make Christian salvation superfluous or to be a substitute for the same, but simply to heal a person and place him, or reinstate him, in "pura naturalia." "Analysis seeks to eliminate repressions and drive-frustrations, remove neurosis, and let 'the normal' function." The function of the analytical care of souls is fulfilled when, free from the hindering obstruction of the drive, it can employ the implications of salvation.[1] In other words, when the analytical care of the soul is completed, then genuine soul cure can take place.

From the foregoing it is obvious that an effort is made to limit the functions of analysis, and when one reads Pfister, one is led to think of this limitation as being so far-reaching as to require a re-examination of the function of the pastor: Should he enlarge his function so as to include the domain of the physician and the psychiatrist, or should he stay within the field which has been his from of old? From a Christian standpoint, it has never been denied that there are mental abnormalities that require the services of a physician. And if psychoanalysis should prove itself to be an indispensable aid to the physician's mental cases, where the pastor is unable to help, certainly Christian theology can have no objection. In this matter the analyst must deal directly with the physician. It is also possible that psychoanalysis may be of service in the more complex aspects of mental disorder, where the pastor is helpless. If the pastor should so enlarge his practice or extend his function so as to include this "roughing in," is a practical question with regard to the division of labor.

As the first chapter of this treatise indicates, the problem is not quite as simple as this. Unless the line of demarcation between soul cure and ordinary medical care is entirely erased, this division of labor is not easily accomplished in the sense that cases suited for analysis are clearly indicated. Pfister's thesis confirms this. The situation becomes grave when one considers that analysis insists on reserving for itself qualitatively important cases involving repressions depending on religio-moral mental conflict. It attempts to treat mental distress as a psychosomatic ailment, when indications are that the problem should be attacked from a religious and moral angle. It simply wants to seek out and dismiss the assertions of the drives without any worry as to conscience. Pfister himself admits this: "If the repressions are too strong and inclusive . . . one must resort to analysis which is not primarily concerned with conscience, but which simply looks for the subjugated drives. In serious cases this is the only way to relieve conscience of the dangerous effects of moral demand and in this manner expedite mental health."[2] In other words, analytical soul cure is most expeditiously carried out when the mentally depressed person gets his eyes opened to a necessary cause and effect relationship conditioned by conscience.

From a Christian point of view one must not overlook that actual care of souls may be involved here. The presupposition of the natural sciences, which includes every event or phenomenon under necessary concatenation of cause and effect, may have religious significance. Pfister could very well have resorted to this as his defense. Of course, had he done so, the border between "analytical" soul care and ordinary pastoral care would have been obliterated. At this point we are confronted with two considerations. On the one hand, we have the dire moral possibility of resolving one's life in terms of the explanations and excuses of naturalism, and on the other, one's religious liberation from an agonized conscience in terms of beholding the past, not for the purpose of excuses, but in the light of divine forgiveness. Unless the necessity of nature is seen in the light of this divine background there can be no religious liberation. But where this background is taken into consideration, natural law may be a preparatory aid in keeping that moral law at a distance, which, as Luther said, is a genuine devil in the conscience.

However, psychoanalysis eliminates this background. And because of this, the exemption from guilt which is granted to the morally struggling person by a deterministic outlook, becomes a real danger to his spiritual health and a threat to his religio-moral future.

But, how about it if there is nothing else to do to eliminate repression? Is there really no other way to put an end to repression bounded in a strong moral conflict than that of pschoanalysis? To affirm this would be to base one's thinking on unproved assertions. First and foremost, "the repression" itself is surrounded by entirely too much mysticism. The concept of the unconscious is itself obscure; there are certainly many degrees of "consciousness" in the evil hotbed of the soul. In the second place, it has not been demonstrated that repression cannot be stopped by other means than analysis. In the previous discussion another way has already been pointed out: the synthetic-analytic power of the moral personality. This is the picture: either technical analysis must become only a subordinated tool in the process of waking the personal life, or become a substitute for the purest and most intense release, which is personal. And one may most certainly say that psychoanalysis as a substitute for religion is a symptom of the *dearth* of adequate personalities in the church and in present-day culture in general.

The same situation obtains when Pfister in his second assertion maintains that analysis does not intend to go beyond the restoring of a person to the naturally "normal." Analysis should merely be preparatory. After it has fulfilled this function, actual soul nurture may begin. "Analysis strives for salvation merely in a biological sense."[3]

In one way or another it is the pastor in the analyst that now claims his right. (Pfister is himself a pastor.) Undoubtedly he is aware of the religious risk involved in psychoanalytical dabbling with religion. And yet he cannot escape being bothered by a dual health ideal for the one who suffers from moral conflict. He who is secretly pressed by guilt must be made biologically normal before one may "speak religion" with him. He must not be made *conscious of his guilt*, that guilt from which he now suffers unconsciously. On the contrary he is to be convinced that the unconscious sense of guilt from which he suffers is really superfluous.

In the preceding discussion it has already become evident that there may be some reason for this procedure. It can be an act of genuine soul care. Where neurosis erects formidable roadblocks in the way of the gospel, and where resources for the stimulation and integration of personal powers are wanting, occasions may arise where nothing better than analysis is available to break down the hindrances. But danger is imminent for the pastor who engages in the practice of psychoanalysis; he may be tempted to extend this pracice to any and all sorts of cases. Pfister's recounting of the many and varying cases to which analysis may be applied indicates this. Moreover, as already indicated, there is the risk in "the normal" into which the analyst has reinstated the person; it is quite possible that the cure is worse than the disease and marks a retrogression. What is decisive here is that the psychoanalytical notion of mental normality and health—harmony of emotional drives—does not coincide with the Christian point of view.[4]

Because Christianity knows health and harmony in larger areas and at deeper levels and from this judges the degree of abnormality, it could very well be that it can better indicate disharmony and an active moral conflict, and do this in a more normal manner and as a better way to spiritual health, as compared with the lax harmony ensuing upon the discovery of the Oedipus complex. Somehow psychoanalysis does not see that the higher spiritual life may be that which is operating the biological and mentally abnormal. "To let the normal operate" before the religio-moral life shall begin; to eliminate the sense of guilt and agony of conscience by a cause and effect psychological regression to extra-ethical causes before Christian salvation, which is simply moral salvation extended to the sufferer, this is to fall for a biological concept of human life, and to commit an outrage against the life of the spirit.

It is a praiseworthy tendency in Pfister that he does not wish to replace Christian salvation with analytical salvation. But since he, nevertheless, and to the great extent his writings indicate, seeks to resolve religio-moral conflicts psychoanalytically, his analysis threatens to be a substitute for Christianity.

At this stage it seems appropriate to ask: What is missing in the psychoanalytical deliverance? The answer is obvious: The profound moral seriousness which can be satisfied only with the most profound liberation. What is wanting is a consciousness of the radically evil in human nature.

Nothing so disturbs the psychoanalyst as does the pessimism of Christianity in reference to sin.

It is the old story! It is the offense of the Cross! No one has so pointedly called this to our attention as did Nietzsche: "Dionysius against the crucified: there is the contradiction," he announces. He puts himself on the side of Dionysius. Nevertheless, Nietzsche is considerably more of a Christian than are the majority of psychoanalysts, who have learned immeasurably more from him than they would admit—except one thing: salt that smarts in the open wound, the struggle, the suffering, the defeat, and the yielding to a person of higher stature. Psychoanalysis as a substitute for religion has been satisfied with surface happiness and harmony, something which Nietzsche despised simply because he was aware of a deeper meaning in man's life, and had a perspective oriented to eternity. Psychoanalysis places unduly modest demands upon happiness. It is to be harmony of all instinctive affections. Christianity, on the other hand, recognizes no other harmony than that in which moral demand is part of the basic agreement. It measures the depth and height of the ideal of happiness in terms of the strength of moral seriousness. It is the criterion Em. af Geijerstam seeks to know about in order to differentiate between different qualities in the "surrender drive"; he declares, namely, that we "in our present position have no sure criterion by which to know when a given expression of energy is sexual or not."[5] The most profound devotion is that which dares to appear in the open under the scrutiny of conscience and under the control of a keen moral consciousness. Psychoanalysis aims at health and harmony on different levels, even a health of the soul, the sort that bears the seal of death on its forehead. In so far as a moral factor, a matter of conscience, is involved in the nervous agony, it is better and testifies to an existence that is nobler and of greater human worth to suffer anxiety than to exercise one's drive *without sensing any conflict*. It evidences a higher spiritual status to belong to the sick who need help than to the healthy who need no physician.

The analysts seem quite willing to admit this when it is a matter of judging human worth in the victims of neurosis.[6] But they ought also to be more considerate in this respect when they assume the delicate assignment of helping the spiritually afflicted so as not to hasten the patient to a health that is worse than the illness itself. This is the risk run by psychoanalysis. It may happen that a person may be set free and made harmonious by analysis, and at the same time have his wings clipped spiritually, and be liberated from a conflict which actually could have brought him more deeply into the seriousness as well as the joy of life. I have seen examples of such analytically "saved" wing-clipped persons.

As a rule psychoanalysis has taken the cue for

its ideal of health from medical men and psychiatrists when it has entered the field of the practice of soul cure. This means that, in reference to man and his possibilities, its demand has been too modest. It is quick to remove the fulcrum that would aid man forward and upward, namely, moral seriousness and moral conflict. It is a misconception that such conflicts are totally evil, and ought to be eliminated by an apologetic clarification. The continually renewed solution of the moral "endopsychic conflict" and sense of guilt in a life of forgiveness is, in the final analysis, the condition for all human spiritual progress. The guilt complex is the explosive with which the human spirit blasts its way into the hard granite of reality. If these conflicts are resolved psychoanalytically, this explosive energy will discharge itself in devious ways, and be dissipated without doing the intended blasting.

After one of his lectures, Pfister mentioned in passing that he was very anxious, in his psychoanalytic treatment of artists, not to eliminate more repressions than necessary; the artist needs the repressions for his artistic creativeness. This is an extraordinary and interesting concession, however serious it might be for the practice of psychoanalysis. Of course, we are not all artists, but we are in this world as creative beings, to do something with our lives. We, too, need the repressions! We need moral battles! We need the sense of guilt!

Considering surface waves of lesser importance, Christianity desires, by means of the guilt conflict, to reach harmony at a much deeper level. *The guilt conflict must not be removed from this earth!* It must be deepened and sharpened, by being laid open before the face of a loving Father. Our sense of guilt is sick because His countenance is lost from our sight. It has become nervousness. For this reason it must be cleansed and be made conscious again. It is curious that it never becomes truly pure and conscious except through forgiveness. This is a psychological fact. Profound sense of guilt is related to faith in forgiveness. The sense of guilt is healthy when the guilt is forgiven and is allowed to live in the sunlight of God's love. The paradox is obvious.

Human life may be observed from two points of view. The one is that of the natural sciences, the analyzing, cause and effect view. This view does not consider responsibility, sin, and guilt. It cannot see it. It explains everything and excuses everything: the act, the will, mental attitudes and man's very being. Man is made up of heredity and environment, and cannot be otherwise than he is. A person may apply this outlook to himself and heartily excuse himself. However, there is another view: one may permit the impenetrable causal relationship itself to point the foil of responsibility at one's self and let the intricate web of one's own life, as it is related to a wider relationship and continuity, eventuate into consciousness of increased guilt. We are prone to follow the first of these two ways. Who among us is able honestly to sense: guilty in all respects! That road has been trod by Another. No one has seen so much of the guilt, His own together with the common guilt of mankind, as He who went to the cross of Golgotha.

We ought not to pride ourselves about any deep penetration into the lower levels of man's inner life and the conflicts thus discovered, nor over any important contribution in the resolving of man's problems of guilt. On the contrary, it is well enough if we can keep our conflicts alive and healthy, so they in turn may keep us from being carried along into superficiality. But if it comes to a decision as to what is the most wholesome life: to assume responsibility, to enter into conflicts and conquer these, or save one's self by excuses—who would hesitate as to his choice in the presence of Jesus Christ?

NOTES AND REFERENCES
[1] Pfister, *Analytische Seelsorge,* p. 139 f.
[2] *Op cit.,* p. 56.
[3] Pfister, *Die Psychanalyt. Methode,* p. 457.
[4] Cf. Hadfield: *Psychology and Morals,* p. 102.
[5] *Medicinsk revue,* 1922, p. 118.
[6] Cf. Strömme: *Nervösitet,* p. 11.

VII

PSYCHOANALYTICAL AND CHRISTIAN "MORALITY OF ADAPTATION," "SELF-REALIZATION"

THE POSITION BASED on a healthy sense of guilt and the doctrine of forgiveness is the point of departure for Christianity as it offers to solve the ethical problem. Psychoanalysis became aware of this problem when it took up its position on the side of the drive of self-dedication and attacked the moral order of the day. The query became this: How can moral law be kept from becoming "legalistic" and "repressing," or how can the absolute and radical moral demand become consistent with a necessary relativism in the concrete demands of morality? From the point of view of religion it has been shown above to what extent psychoanalysis is justified in raising its voice in favor of "freedom from the law." It has been aware of the pressure of legalism and the imminent peril in which the freedom of allegiance finds itself, a freedom like that of Christian allegiance. But psychoanalysis can be equally well understood, and its good intentions acknowledged, when in the name of morality it goes to war against "the law." It can explain that it is not the law as such that it would fight, but a morality that does not fit the case, that is not "adapted" to man's prerequisites and for this reason is not an operating morality.

Psychoanalysis implies that moral demands must be suited to man's resources, or that man must adapt himself to the demands he puts on himself in line with his ability and according to the conditions and laws of life. "The ideal must not be set too high, because if it is, it will prevent Eros from becoming articulate in the conduct of life, and must spend its life in the limbo of the repressed complex. An ideal that is too restraining makes man unfit for life—just as too tight a rein checks the speed of the horse. Again it must not be too weak, which condition would lead to a recrudescence of lust, making man socially unfit—the horse running away. Rather, a loving adherence to the reality of life is man's normal and happiest adjustment to life . . . *In order to conquer neurosis one must arrive at a transformation of personality, the creation of a new control in and of the life of the patient, according to an ideal of life adjusted to the demands of life and human nature.*"[1]

Extraordinarily difficult problems are here involved. And it may not be too much to say that psychoanalysts as such are not quite up to what is required, a matter in which they are not alone.

111

They have not comprehended the nature nor the presuppositions of ethical adaptation and, consequently, run the risk of undermining morality itself, while at the same time they desire to shield morality from legalistic disintegration. The expression just cited from Bratt brings to light the shortcomings of his insight in the problems of ethical adaptation, at the same time as it gives a glimpse of a solution to the problem. This also applies to a statement by Hadfield. He says: "It follows from these principles *that every age has to some extent a distinct moral standard.* Different countries, different customs; different ages, different ethics. So what is right for one phase and for one age is wrong for another. Pugnacity may be smiled at in a boy of twelve; condemned in a man of thirty. It is right for a man of forty, in the interests of justice, to speak the truth even against his best friend; the cause of truth must take precedence even over the interests of individuals. For a boy of fourteen it is better to withhold the truth than to betray his comrades, for that is the age for the development of heroic loyalty. The boy who will sneak at thirteen will later in life basely betray his cause and country. Since every age has its distinctive psychology it is very necessary not to impose a false standard at any specific age."[2]

One is not sure as to what adaptation or compromise in ethical matters involves. What is it that justifies or necessitates relativity in ethical demands? Does it demand a compromise of morality itself, of the demands of truth, righteousness, honor, integrity, goodness, love, so that it shall ever be: You must, according to your circumstances, your age, your status of development, be relatively integrious, relatively honest, etc.? Anyone can see that such moral adaptation is impossible, and can lay no claim to moral standing. He who has acquired such moral relativism has acquired a falsified and corrupt moral consciousness. That love proceeds pedagogically in its demands does not alter morality itself, as if it concerned a different morality for different ages. It would be a very peculiar rearing indeed, if a lad thirteen years of age were to learn that group loyalty or loyalty to his gang were to supersede truth itself and other ethical norms, and then later would have to have this concept corrected. A teacher must *understand* and respect a youth's loyalty toward his group, but he betrays him if he does not at the same time give him to understand the limitations within which this group solidarity is valid, and further makes clear to him that group loyalty is subordinate to a higher loyalty. Moreover, a relativism exemplified by the following quotation is similarly objectionable: "It is *better* to live in a permanent love relationship with *one* unmarried young woman than to have sexual relations with several, although it is *best* to live in continence before marriage." Any and all moral concepts that come in the form of such graduated stages must be repudiated both pedagogically as well as on general principles, regardless of the attitude of the *community* in reference to such relativity. Relativism of this sort in the name of *morality* destroys the radical demands involved in notions of a totally integrated personality: "Become a person different from what you are." This is present in every ethical demand. Bratt is quite right: Whenever a person is confronted by a moral demand, an appeal is made to a personality change according to the moral problem involved.

It is undoubtedly true of Hadfield, as the case with the majority of the better psychologically trained pedagogues, that moral demands and rules of right and wrong are confused. Rules of behavior cannot successfully exact moral demands in the inward parts. They will have to be satisfied with surface obedience, and are in no position to punish evil intents that are not translated into word and deed. And if these rules become too rigorous, they result in negative reactions and transgressions which cannot be prosecuted, and which tend to undermine justice itself. This has been amply demonstrated by laws and regulations passed during times of crisis. Rather than being successfully enforced, they have caused open wounds in both general regulations as well as in morality itself. Obviously, rules of conduct will have to change and vary with the conditions in which they have their reference. But morality cannot participate in such variation.

Nevertheless a certain relativism does obtain in the moral demand as it relates itself to the conditions of everyday living. But that which motivates and justifies this relativism is something else again. This is to be found in the necessity for some sort of limitation upon the scope or range of the moral demand. "Thou must serve thy neighbor" or "Thy life and work must be in the service of mankind," are moral demands in point. Such unlimited moral demands put upon man who himself stands in a very limited relationship with the content and context of history and all the ramifications of mankind, must of necessity be limited to the circumscribed situation and possibilities in which the given person finds himself. Who formulates the limitation and makes the situation endurable for him who conscientiously seeks to fulfill his duties in a world of endless obligations? Here one must consider the existence of divine love, a love which is the genesis of the moral demand, and which is mindful of him to whom the duty is given.

The "call" or "calling" is the matrix in which Christian ethics places the complex of factors involved in this relativism and the adaptation. From one point of view, the "call" is the limitation God in His love bestows on each person's mission in life. Space here does not permit one to enter into detail upon the problem and queries this concept involves. Its history is long and complicated. Suffice it to state in this context, that the *call* does not imply haggling or bargaining so far as the moral demand is concerned. Its "radicalism," its insistence upon total dedication, will, attitude, goodness, love, and unselfishness, has not diminished with the limitation upon the particular mission. Rather, the demand is bound to God's fatherly care for him to whom it is directed; it is enveloped in the love of Him who watches over and has compassion for His child; it is calculated and measured out for each one by Him who is also prepared to raise up and embrace those who fail.

I notice that many psychoanalysts are either aware of, or suspect, some such solution to the problem of adaptation as the only way out. They vaguely suggest a condition in which morality is not "dangerous," simply because the person himself, through the manner in which the moral demand approaches him, becomes committed to more than the demand, and becomes, as it were, compromised to the advantage of him who makes the demand. From this it should be obvious that psychoanalysis, in its morality of adaptation, by and large gropes about for another moral situation than that which we ordinarily assume to obtain in the moral milieu of the community. It is unfortunate indeed that psychoanalysis must resort to moral haggling—lowering the moral standard—in order to achieve the necessary adaptation.

Again it must be said: It is God alone and His love behind the demand that can maintain the standard under circumstances of moral limitation. He, and He alone, makes relativism possible in the moral demand without affecting the moral standard.

Adaptation is the motto of psychoanalytical ethics. To this is added, "self-realization." Unless the ethical demand is adapted to the conditions set up by the individual, morality becomes an outrage against man's "self"; morality becomes immoral. Poul Bjerre states: "It is characteristic of the morality constructed on the foundations of modern psychology that it does not basically have a normative setting applicable to all men, except the general notion of self-realization. Every norm must, so to speak, be worked out from the individual's own prerequisites, and its function is not to bring pressure on his powers and capacities, but to assist them toward liberation. In this manner the peril which morality peradventure formerly implied is obviated. At the same time morality has increased in ethical worth. Ways and means for our adaptation to the eternal order come about in a larger measure."[3]

This concern for moral autonomy is, of course, a legitimate interest. Peculiarly enough, it would appear from reading Bjerre, Bratt, et al., that the Christian ethic has never interested itself in this matter. And yet it is basically in this very interest that the evangelical ethic differentiates itself from the Roman ethic. Psychoanalysis and Christianity can never come to any mutual understanding on this point any more than on the other; that is, as long as the former so completely avoids further cognizance of the latter before it enters into a critique thereof in terms of the efforts made within the area of Christian ethics to solve the religio-ethical problem of freedom.

By this there is definitely no intention on my part to infer that if there were a desire toward mutual understanding, complete unity would be attained. If such were the case, then mutual interest in moral autonomy, and interest in morality in terms of self-realization, could shift the discussion to the problem around which everything finally revolves, namely the question as to the implications and possibilities involved in self-realization. What is this self that is to be realized? That it is man's "potentialities as a human,"[4] Christian ethics can accept. But what are these potentialities? Are they the human potentialities of Nietzsche's superman,

Kant's rational man, or Christianity's man of faith? It is, of course, true, is it not, that man should "make the most possible of his life"?[5] But how is this brought about? What is it that brings about the realization of the deeper forces in man? Is it the spontaneous psychic healing force which, as far as is feasible, should be left to itself? Is it the "psycho-synthetic tendency" which in its drift-like function needs but a negative assistance in terms of the removal of hindrances to its spontaneous activity? Or is it necessary that the hindrances and resistance be removed in such a manner that in the same process certain powers are brought to life which otherwise would have remained dormant? Or perhaps positive interference from the outside is indicated, and if so, what would it be?

The answer to this query was given above when I made reference to the revitalizing forces of personality, the *law* and *gospel* of personality. Because, unless the personal life, which kindles life, is both—law and gospel—it helps not at all to make the most possible of one's life. It is the personal unity of law and gospel, of a request and a gift, of a claim and a capacity, which will aid man toward self-realization in the sense that in the very encounter with the revitalizing personal life is created, from "the potentialities," *the self* that is to be realized. Really profound self-realization always has the characteristic of a creative act and rebirth.

And the more tenaciously this act takes hold, the more serious becomes the ethical implication. Man does not realize himself and his greatest possibilities by placing before himself an ideal that flatters his drives. To imply that the command, "thou shalt," if it "goes contrary to our instincts and feelings" becomes "a strange intruder in our soul"[6] is to place a low value on man's potentialities. Just such a "thou shalt" presented in the form of a person has of necessity a place in man's noblest and most profound self-realization. It concerns the encounter with the awakening of *everything* powerful and noble in the personal life, not just the mere *encounter* with the person of Christ. In every serious apprehension of the kindling of our greatest potentialities by another person we experience something of what in Christian terminology is called rebirth, or which in other Christian verbiage is called forgiveness of sins. Every profound personal impression purges and cleanses like a bath of remorse; indeed it is actually an experience of genuine remorse out of which the self emerges as a new being. The secret included in the forgiveness of sins is, in a richer measure, the same as the secret of all intimate personal fellowship.

Christianity, too, aims at self-realization. However, it takes account of possibilities and potentialities of the self, quite different from those of psychoanalysis. For this reason it puts greater emphasis on the moral demand. It knows only too well that the most genuine in man's "self" is not innocent of "the law's demands," but on the contrary out of the depths shouts its "Yes" to them. Moreover, the encounter with the absolute demand in personal representation involves renewed energy to endure the demand without making of the drives treacherous and hidden enemies.

NOTES AND REFERENCES

[1] I. Bratt: *Splittring och enhet*, p. 92 ff.
[2] *Psykologi och moral*, page 125.
[3] In his Foreword to Hadfield: *Psychology and Morals*.
[4] Poul Bjerre: *Korset och livsbägaren*, p. 28.
[5] *Op. cit.*
[6] Poul Bjerre: *Op. cit.*, p. 55.

VIII

SUBLIMATION. THE SOUL. THE DIVINE

IN VARIOUS WAYS we have now attempted to arrive at the pivotal point in the psychology of psychoanalysis, or to the point where the psychological philosophy implies or presupposes a notion of what life in itself, in its noblest manifestation and in its very essence, is. The idea of self-realization, with which we have just been wrestling, inquiringly directs our attention back to the self and to the soul, and to the secrecy which conceals itself behind its "potentialities." Psychoanalysis also includes in its theory and practice a notion about the essence of life, a "philosophy of life," regardless of how eagerly some may attempt to deny it. It is a philosophy of life which cannot come to terms with the Christian persuasion. It is for this reason: that which is a personally spiritual reality for Christianity, psychoanalysis transforms into impersonal forces. The lack of ethical content, something of which I have accused psychoanalysis, is simply a descriptive expression in reference to this concept of the essence of life as an impersonal flow of energy.

As far as psychoanalysis is concerned, man is but a given quantum of psychosomatic energy. "Each person has at his disposal just so much of the energy of life."[1] Of course, this energy can be put into the service of various drives, higher or lower. It may be sublimated or put into service by the primary functions of the drive. What should concern mankind is the proper use of *the given*.

This impersonal trend of thought circumvents the pivotal point of the Christian concept. God is not satisfied with "the given" in man. He demands something new and creates the new. The creative spiritual aptitudes which are released are not a given quantum of energy doled out to everyone and reserved in the subconscious. There are inexhaustible resources in the love of the living God, and His encounter with man is not a matter of bringing antithetical drives into harmony, but the recreating of a new life.

What should be clear is that theology must not let itself be duped by the fact that psychoanalysis with strong verbiage and idealistic efforts occasionally sets itself in opposition to the materialism of the day. When some psychoanalyst cries out that contemporary man has forgotten he has a soul, it appears as if this were a sign of a spiritual awakening and the blowing of a fresh breeze. What should be noted here is a reaction against an older stubborn medical materialism, and a reaffirmation that it is the mind that is at work in life's process of deterioration as well as in its rebirth. Undoubtedly, there is something of real worth in this reaction against the older practice within medical science. Most certainly the soul plays a very much greater role even where bodily ills are concerned than physicians hitherto have been willing to admit. But Christianity and theology must not be overwhelmingly moved by this revived insight. In general, a deep abyss separates this concept of the soul from the strictly Christian idea. "The life stream" or "life energy" still bears the name of *psychic* energy, sexuality changes unnoticeably to "psychosexuality," and between the lowest notion of libido and the highest form of life there are at its best merely degrees of difference. The confusion caused by this indiscriminate blending of the physical and the spiritual, and the general muddle of sensuality involved in the concept of the soul, is rather well portrayed by the psychoanalytical doctrine of sublimation.

This doctrine is not something appended and unessential, so that psychoanalysis might be able to do without it; on the contrary, it is basic in its psychology. Without the presuppositions supporting this doctrine, the whole theory concerning sexuality or any other drive denoting life energy would be impossible. The doctrine of sublimation has the function of explaining how all the energies and drives have emerged from the original drive namely, sexuality. A "lower, coarser" sexual energy has been sublimated to a "higher, finer" energy by means of the intervening sublimation and developmental factors. And thus, finally, from this sexual energy have come the highest spiritual creations of culture. This one thing is obvious: the factual phenomena of life would be unexplainable in terms of sexuality or some other generic drive as the genesis of life's various manifestations, were it not for this doctrine of sublimation.

Moreover, this doctrine is also a necessary background for the theory of suppression, and is most definitely essential in the placing of this theory in its proper context. Sublimation as differentiated from repression is taken to be the proper resolving of conflicts between the drives and the obstacles in the way of these drives—obstacles that in the name of culture and morality have been erected against free expression of the drives. Now where it becomes necessary to restrain a given drive, the restraint is to be in terms of sublimation rather than repression; of necessity the drive must spend itself, and may do so in this unhindered sublimated form. If on the other hand, it is not allowed thus to spend itself, it is driven inward to the unconscious where it poisons the very center of one's being. And again, from another point of view, if it is not allowed to spend itself in a sublimated form, it will not tend toward a rise from nature to culture.

Obviously the whole theory of psychoanalysis stands or falls with the doctrine of sublimation. This gives paramount importance to a thorough investigation of sublimation.

I shall begin with a lengthy citation from Freud, a citation in which his concept of the sexual nature of life energy or the libido comes into clear view in his presentation of sublimation. He writes: "Libido is an expression taken from the doctrine of the emotions. This is the term we have applied to the quantitative, even if as yet unmeasurable, energy associated with such emotions as are involved in everything that may be included in the expression *love*. The very core of what we call love constitutes, as a matter of course, that which we usually call love and which poets sing about, namely sex love and which has sex union as its goal. But we do not distinguish this from other expressions which participate in the generic term *love*, as for example, self-love, parental love, the love of children for parents, general friendship, and love for mankind, or devotion to concrete objects and abstract ideas. Our justification for this lies in this that psychoanalytical research has taught us that all of these strivings are expressions of exactly those emotional drives which strive to bring about sexual intercourse, but which when this definite generic goal is not in view, are restrained from this purpose. However, enough of the basic essence is retained so as to make its generic identity recognizable. . . . What we imply here is that the connotations of the word *love* are so well rooted in the denotative use of the term that we can do no better than to use the expression in all of its connotations as a basis for our scientific clarifications and presentations."[2] With this broadening of the meaning of the term love, so Freud implies, psychoanalysis has not set up anything original. "According to Plato, in reference to its origin, activity, and relation, Eros evidences complete identity with the psychoanalytical notion of the love power, libido; and when the apostle Paul in his renowned letter to the Corinthians praises love above everything, it is clear that he has conceived of love in said 'broadened' meaning."[3] Freud adds that he could just as easily have used the words *eros* or *eroticism* in place of sexuality, but this would have been a concession to those who consider sexuality as something shameful!

Even with Freud, consequently, there appears to be a distinction between different kinds of "love": sex drive, finer spirtual love, culture-creating eros of every kind. The several forms of love imply a "desexualized" content. Of course all varieties, according to Freud's point of view, come from the generic sex drive, or that drive which would eventuate in sexual intercourse. But all of them retain

127

"enough of the basic essence so as to make their generic identity recognizable." Accordingly, the libido is in all of its manifestations as life energy the original groping basic drive directed towards sexual communion. The sexual continues as the center, as does the libido, the latter not being in and of itself a complete sex drive, but constituting the drive which tends toward and has its consummation in sex union. It is important to establish that this drive which tends toward sex communion constitutes for Freud the main content in "love." Eros, parental love, "culture love," are sublimations of this drive. It is, therefore, quite incorrect when Freud says that he could just as well have used the word "eros" as libido or sexuality. On the contrary, this usage would have been impossible for him, since eros, according to his point of view, originates in sexuality and is sublimated or desexualized. Therefore one must not permit oneself to be led astray when Freud declares the libido to be the same as the German word "lieben," to love, and means that his "pan-sexualism" consequently contains a very inclusive concept of love, and is not so dangerous. Sexualism is, nevertheless, patently the all-governing notion since, in the final analysis, it is from the sexual that what is called love and culturally creative power originates.

However, it is calculated that by means of sublimation the libido shall become something nobler.

Now, how does sublimation come about? It comes about in this manner, that the libido mass meets resistance that would set up a road block. The consequence of such a collision can be one of the two following: either the desire residing in the drive is repressed into the unconscious where it remains as a threatening unsatisfied wish, which from time to time sends symptoms into the conscious life, and brings about psychical disturbances of various kinds; or the drift mass may be so received by the censoring resistance as to be allowed to pass, at least in part, through the gate of the censor. On the other side of this passage it appears as a sublimated drive, as eros, as something artistically creative, as ambition to explore, as social love, etc.[4]

A whole list of questions arise out of this. How is this spiritual "filtration" to be conceived? What is this resistance, which checks the flow of the drive mass and which exercises censure and serves as a "filtering apparatus"? How has this resistance or this inner power factor come into being, if that which is originally in man is after all only the libido or sexuality? Is the censoring factor itself a result of sublimation? But in this case, how was this first sublimation made possible, that is, before there was anything else besides the libido, and before there was any censor formed within man which could check and sublimate the drive? Or in other words: Is this censoring factor itself to be looked upon as a higher creature of culture, and whence does it as such originate?

It is not always easy to find clear answers to these questions from the psychoanalysts. As a rule, the problem and the difficulties presented by Christian thought in reference to this presentation have not been definitely fixed. The inference is that one is talking about something self-evident when one deals with the deviation of sexual energy from its original goal and direction in favor of other goals and assignments, as if this energy could be transformed as to its contents according to the goals it chances to hit upon or catches sight of in the objective world. Freud speaks of a "reconstruction" (or construction) from sex energy itself (during the latent sex period of childhood) of spiritual powers which later will stand in the way of restraining the sex drive and, as it were, confining this drive in a narrower channel. These restraints are in terms of disgust, sense of shame, esthetic and moral demands. He speaks of this as if it were a self-evident matter, easily understood, in spite of the fact that it is quite odd that out of the sexual energy mass suddenly can emerge a moral and esthetic censor which is able to check or hinder the free flow of this energy mass.

The difficulty involved in the concept of sublimation thus arises as soon as one raises the question as to how it is possible for a censor able to control sexual energy in man to emerge out of the all-powerful sexual energy itself. As Scheler has pointed out, it appears as if Freud is not aware that at this juncture the argument moves in a vicious circle. It is a case of begging the question, as it is assumed that one already has at hand that reality, the origin of which one seeks to explain.

However, it is in this connection that psychoanalysis has developed its doctrine *the ego* and *the superego*. These have been inserted as subject in the censor. How are these to be understood, and how shall their appearance in the arena be explained? At this point I shall adhere rather closely to the exegesis by the faithful disciple of Freud, Franz Alexander. He depicts the relationship between the *the ego* and *the superego* as follows: "The ego of the cultured man appears before us as a figure differentiated into two parts, divided as to functions. Originally it was a homogeneous unified organ of observation for outer and inner stimuli. Its dynamic purpose was to bring the results of the inner observations, that is, the demands of the drives, into harmony with reality—that is, reality on the outside; in brief, it should serve to satisfy the drives. While it—the ego—has not only retained but also greatly further developed its power of observation toward the outside, it has lost a great deal of its power of observation inwardly, or more correctly, surrendered it to regions of the unconscious. Not all the inner drive powers manage to reach the conscious, but only those that have passed the port of censure of the inner organ of observation. Thus the function of the personality's inward observation was restricted. From here on its function is to provide for the satisfaction of the demands of those drives that have crossed the border of repression. The other part of the demand of the drive does not, generally speaking, come under its domain because it has already been turned back as indisputable and loathsome in terms of reality; that is, it is being repressed. Thus it happens that many of the inner restraining events remain unconscious, yes, even the large part of the restraint of moral conscience. The inner censor has assumed the role of a conscious judging function, in that it has stereotyped the results of earlier once conscious verifications of reality."[5]

In order to understand sublimation it is, however, patently necessary to get a better understanding of the *ego censor* so that, if possible, it shall become comprehensible that the passage through this censor has such a sublimating effect. According to the presentations made by the analysts this depends largely upon the censorship of the superego. The superego is the unconsciously functioning inner authority which is identical to the prohibitions and commandments which the child has received from his parents during the early years. It is, to use Freud's verbiage, "the representative of our relationship to our parents. As small children we knew, admired, feared these higher beings; later we made them part of ourselves. Considered more precisely, the superego is the heir of the Oedipus Complex. Essentially it is a moral censor."[6]

Now, it is not really quite well understood that we have adopted the parental authority and made it an inner judging and censuring authority, of which authority we originally could take no account, except in terms of the factors invoked by psychoanalysis, namely, the drift mass and its integrating representative in the *ego* on the one hand, and the milieu in which we live, next to the influence of our parents, on the other. How is it really possible on the presupposition of merely these two factors to "take on" the parental authority, and make it into an inner organ of reaction? In this connection a new concept is readily inserted, namely, "identification." The child identifies himself with his prototype, with his authority. But this new concept neither clarifies nor adds intelligibility to anything; it is merely a paraphrase of the "subsumption" of the parental authority or the prototype. The question persists how this subsumption or identification is psychologically possible. At least there must be some one who subsumes or identifies himself, that is, a third factor which makes possible and explains the "subsumption," the identification, and likewise the sublimation. One must take account of a sensitive apparatus of subsumption in man *from the start,* otherwise it becomes unintelligible how the "superego" could come into being. This is undoubtedly what secretly takes place in psychoanalysis, and what makes its reasoning seem so self-evident; quite unnoticed an original third something is smuggled in between the drift mass and the milieu, a third factor which makes it possible for the collision between the drive and the milieu to result in a moral organ in man. Without notice an already existing moral factor is injected, the origin of which one would like to explain. Moreover, to this factor is ascribed the power to sublimate. Without it the qualitative transformation of the drift energy would be unintelligible in every case. How otherwise can the drift energy become a higher form of love or eros simply by being "strained" through a narrower passage, that is, if the guard at the passage himself is of such a nature that he is able to employ the energy in a higher service?[7]

Here we are touching upon a problem of greater general interest than that offered by the theory of sublimation set forth by psychoanalysis. It is a question concerning the origin of morality. However difficult the fact of morality itself may appear, it is nevertheless easily established that the moral ego is something which successively and gradually comes into being in a person or in mankind. Mankind has required a long history to arrive at the sort of "conscience" it today evidences at its best. And in the individual person's life we note a similar development. Is it not evident that the moral ego is a product of development, a product which in one way or another comes into being through a union of man's "developmental tendencies" and his environment? And it appears to be the latter which performs the actual work in this process of becoming. Actually now, is it not the milieu which creates the moral ego in the reaction to "the life tendencies"? Is the moral ego anything else than an expression for the reaction of parental authority against the tendencies toward lust in the child, in the final analysis, then, a creation of the social environment? Is not this the very origin of morality, and is not this a disturbing consideration when the enhancement of moral right and unassailability is involved? For is the creating milieu so unassailable? And is there not something quite justified in the basic thinking of psychoanalysis, as well as in the thinking of countless others, that that which has the original life's right to exist, "life tendencies," "developmental tendencies," "the libido," must first of all have freedom to live, and that which has come into being as a later accretion must be considered as a secondary and usable factor?

The reply to these remarks is already given. *If*

the situation is such that the fundamental tendency of life is more or less this sexual will to lust, how may one explain that from this will to lust, or from its carrier, the ego, a moral ego can arise simply by an outside reaction against the lust tendency? Surely in human life itself, even in its earliest stages, there must be a censorship, a *ferment* for moral growth, a factor in man himself, which is being reared, which co-operates in this moral growth, which allows itself to be influenced and acquiesces in its reviving stimulation; a factor which "sublimates" and "identifies" itself; a ferment which contains within itself the enzyme for the highest moral attainment. We are quite familiar with the cause and effect thinking—even though it is as a rule too dogmatic—which lies behind the low esteem in which morality is held by psychoanalysis, as well as by all naturalistic ethics in general. This is the trend of this sort of thinking: nothing can be found in the effect which is not contained in the cause. Now the effect reveals itself: the moral ego has a sufficient "natural" explanation in the union of man's drive life and the milieu. Clearly no higher or divine origin is involved; rather, morality becomes secondary in its relation to life. The notion of cause and effect makes this carefree moral attitude possible. One factor is forgotten, a factor without which the "effect" in question could not be brought about. The logic of the matter is this: the remarkable result which is present in the "effect," namely, the moral ego, especially at its peaks (the life of Jesus for example) surely must indicate that there is something in the cause that would account for this remarkable effect. In every case there must somewhere be found a sufficient cause for this effect, wherever one may have to look for it. In this moral growth there must somewhere be a ferment that can adequately account for the moral possibility. Without this, the law of cause and effect cannot be satisfied. In the face of this unfortunate dilemma, the mind is forced to greater effort, to dig deeper in the "drift life," into "the stream of energy." Seeking for this third creative something, perhaps it must dig itself *through* to something else, something which is not now known as drive or energy alone, but a slumbering or awakening personality life which points beyond itself to something higher.

At this point I cannot in any greater detail enter into a psychological examination of the factors involved in the origin of the moral ego; this must be deferred to a later discussion. However, for the present, this may be asserted: In the general life of man, and in the love life itself, if we take careful note, we encounter not only an original libido drive, but also an original *regulator* of this drive, a regulator which in the process of its function seeks to raise and ennoble the drive, a regulator that possesses a disposition to give commands and prohibitions as well as devotion to a higher order, and would attract (or draw) the sensual devotion into its own sublimating movement. It is of considerable importance to accentuate this, that the "resistance" met from the regulator or "the censor" is not merely law and commandments but a force equipped with powers of sublimation, an agency that in and of itself *can* elevate and ennoble the drive. And if one can discover in life itself an original imperative and elevating power, then two things otherwise incomprehensible can be explained: (1) how the censor of the superego, by means of influence from without, from the milieu, can increase in power and be refined in its reactions; the milieu, parental authority, etc., in this case assist only in the giving of form to the power resident in the rudimentary aptitudes of the life itself; (2) how sublimation is possible. It is made possible by virtue of the presence in life itself of an original elevating force which would raise man as a nature-being above himself and concentrate all his powers in this lofty direction. In other words, there is someone within man that *sublimates*.

It is obvious that this sublimation does not have the characteristic of a physical or chemical process comparable to that of which the psychoanalysts are speaking. It is not a sensual sex energy that is transformed into some kind of finer energy through some complicated process of nature. It is not a coarser energy that is changed into a finer one and which peradventure simultaneously is diluted into a less concentrated mixture. This awesome (dreadful, perhaps) materialistic manner of thinking does not reach even the simplest insight of objective *psychology. What really occurs in sublimation is that a guiding and elevating will, desire, and love, which are already present, engage other powers of life in their service and for their purposes derive energetic auxiliaries from these, and with these subservient powers at their command find their own power growing.*

That such a sublimation, or that such a concentration of energy from various directions within man, can take place is quite beyond doubt. Every instance of unification of will power is in a certain sense a sublimation. The enthusiastic laborer who strives for the improvement of the working conditions of his group is undoubtedly able to sublimate his natural energy; that is to say, he can put this natural energy into service under the guiding, enthusiastic, spiritual-ethical devotional drive and thus reinforce this drive in its urge to spearhead a powerfully organized contingent of energy. The person devoted to the work of solving a difficult theoretical problem may sublimate natural energy in the same manner. He may experience that desires and drives, which otherwise used to present themselves, in the presence of the mental effort and the summons of the will do *not* call for attention as usual, but either absent themselves or soon cease insisting. All his concentrated energy is spent on the assignment. Plans, order, and a unified line of action, are part of his life as long as the concentration continues. He sublimates.

This applies also to that energy which is included in sex life. Literature gives testimony to this—that sexual continence is necessary or profitable, as for example, in concentration upon a prolonged intellectual problem, a scientific assignment, etc. These demand concentrated energy, and not least the energy associated with the sexual drive. Concentration on work assignments sublimates. Here one is not confronted by any impersonal transformation of the drive itself but a taking over of its energy on the part of the subject, when the subject is seeking for contingents of assistance for a definite assignment.

This does not in any sense contradict the observations made by many analysts, observations which have been touched upon in preceding discussions, namely, that devotion to one's occupation and fitness for sexual functioning are associated and move in parallel lines. If the one is in a state of fervor, then this is a symptom that the other also functions in a wholesome fashion. So it is implied. If the one is checked, so is the other. As a basis for this theory we have the rather well substantiated observation that a neurosis which disturbs some aspect of the fervor of life easily disturbs life in general and carries with it a detrimental effect on ambition in one's work as well as on the sex drive. It is also reasonable to suppose that inner concentration or self-reflection which for a longer or shorter duration restrains the neurosis and concentrates energy for a given work assignment will also restore order and remove restraints from the sphere of sexual life. But that this concentration on a work assignment, or that the devotion of the sublimating subject in reference to a work assignment in this manner, brings about wholesomeness and order in the drift life does not imply that therefore the drive must *spend itself,* and that only if it does spend itself will ambition in one's work ensue. Moreover, wholesomeness in the drift life must not only obtain in association with the energetically concentrated and sublimating subject, but must for its continuation have the presupposition that the drive does not spend itself but furnishes energy for the concentration. A wholesome drift life, temperateness in the spending of the drive, and personal concentration or sublimation, are closely related.

Sublimation presupposes a subject which sublimates. This stands out most clearly in the question concerning the ability of Christian faith to give man a definite course of action. Faith would of necessity include everything in this course of action. Luther has made this clear in his writing about the liberty of the Christian man. The free man of faith of necessity sublimates; he cannot do otherwise. But at this point it also becomes clear what energy it is that is primarily made the object of sublimation, and of what spirit the children who sublimate are. The energy which is being sublimated is not in the first place the energy of the natural drives: the sex drive, food getting, etc.; not even the natural energy toward self-preservation, but the energy of spiritual self-preservation. In faith man is free from himself, free from action directed against himself, free from acts upon himself. In faith he gets a new orientation toward God, a theocentric orientation. It carries the deeds along with itself in its activity, the deeds which man otherwise and formerly used in order to advance himself in the sight of God. He is no longer in need of these other deeds. He is set free from his religious egoism, and the energy thus used is set free for other things. But God does not need this liberated energy in any other way than that man by faith shall be carried into the course of action peculiar to divine love, and in this manner be of "assistance" to God in His love for man. It is not the libido which is primarily sublimated; it is love that is sublimated, but, of course, it is a recreated subject of love and faith that sublimates. And that which this subject integrates and sublimates is, in the first place, the forces which have gone astray; but, of course, it also carries with it energies from other sources, even from the sex life, in the measure that the faith of forgiveness attains power and grace to assume moral duties, duties which need, for a longer or shorter period, the energy of life's natural functions.

Psychoanalysis has never really and fully convinced itself as to the activating subject in the process of sublimation. However, in actuality it treats man, who harbors the drive energy, as a toy in the hands of imported notions of the superego and the encountering goals from the outside. The drive energy is taken in hand by these. On the other hand, there are the difficult obstacles of the superego, impersonal objectives and goals, which pull the drive energy out of sensuality and direct it toward itself. This is the conception they set up in reference to the process of sublimation. There is no *subject* that acts within "the energy" itself. But the secret in sublimation, and that which alone makes it meaningful and actual, is the becoming and presence of the sublimating subject itself, the subject which certainly is present even in the censoring "superego," but which, in order to have the power to sublimate *at the same time* is the subject in the self-surrender, but in his surrender is more profound than the drive energy. And never does this subject present itself more clearly crystallized than it does in the Christian faith of forgiveness where the devoted subject has the power to sharpen the censor of the "superego" and its charge before judgment, and yet in the presence of the judgment retain its standing and realize itself as a liberated and independent subject.

For "sublimation" it is demanded that there be a subject that sublimates. And a subject sublimates to the extent that it has been liberated. But to be thoroughly liberated means to be born again, and to be re-created. But to be re-created implies a devotion of the self to the Creator and from Him to obtain the strength rightly to use and spend one's powers in the service of the Creator. *God* "sublimates" in that He makes of man a sublimating subject.

Two ancient words from the history of ethics come to the fore in the sublimation ethics of psychoanalysis: teleology and eudaemonism. Both of these tend, appearance to the contrary notwithstanding, to lead one into most deceptive channels, this largely because under their guise the sublimation of energy does not proceed from an untinctured and redeemed heart.

Psychoanalysis does not really understand the term "soul" in its definitive Christian sense. "Soul" in the latter sense is not to be found before one has passed the borders of the human and arrived at the divine. To have a mutual relationship with

144

God is to possess a "soul"; to break this union with Him is to kill the soul.

Among various psychoanalysts, and in circles closely associated with them, one hears about the self-healing powers in man's soul, analogous to physical self-healing, or about a "psycho-synthetic tendency" or a "progressive tendency" in the soul. There is undoubtedly some truth in this. But in this parallelism of the physical and the mental there is ample room for the presence of an impersonal and therefore an essentially unpsychological way of looking at things. Self-healing analogous to the rebuilding of cells in the body does not take place in the soul. One can speak of a psycho-synthetic tendency, but it is not self-healing in any other sense than that *it reaches out for healing powers in the objective world*. It is a longing which seeks for the object of its longing, a hand that reaches out for help, a soul that *prays*. Thus psycho-synthesis is not self-healing in any other sense. This fact may at times be observed within psychoanalysis itself, or in the psycho-synthesis where the practice has risen to a more personal outlook. For Christianity in general and for the Christian conception of the soul in particular, it is decisive that the saving power which encounters the "progressive tendency" in the soul, that which brings reality to the very longing for restoration, corresponds to the *most intense* longing, the longing of the *"image of*

God," in a person, so that the liberation is not fictitious but real. Moreover, it is most real and effective where the bondage is the greatest, that is, in the preoccupation with one's self in terms of materialistic and spiritual motivation. This cannot take place in one person during one time through one agent, and in another person at another time by some other agent; such release is what we have called fictitious, and at best is merely a smattering of "culture." It is not a developing and inclusive culture which in the course of time continues to extend fresh occasions of release for man's greatest "apriori." And the power to liberate this lies only in that agency in which resides a personal religio-moral life. But in the measure that it actually liberates and realigns the direction of activity at the very center, it is one and the same personal life, one and the same divine life, one and the same "word" which, through varying forms, finds its way to the eye and ear of the soul. But he alone is centrally liberated to a new direction of activity who has been liberated from a life steeped in sheer selfishness, a life that looks out for itself in everything, even in God. In other words, only he who is liberated *ethically* is truly liberated. Only he can "lose his life" in a meaningful and basic sense. Everything depends on this mode of "losing" one's self. Here as anywhere, what does it profit a man, if he gains the whole world and loses his soul?

The soul can live only in ethical release, live personally in the real meaning of the term. And this "personal" cannot be apprehended in the context of impersonal forces. Any such view devaluates man and robs him of that which institutes his mark of nobility: personal responsibility. In his noted lecture on Christianity and crime, given at the ecumenical gathering in Stockholm, president Simons stated: "As I see it, psychoanalysis has placed us in the danger of resolving human guilt and with that also the human soul; of looking on man spiritually and mentally as a complicated natural phenomenon, upon whom one may have influence, but whom one cannot make responsible for his actions."[8]

Psychoanalysis has an impersonal conception of man. Similarly and quite naturally, it has an impersonal notion of God, if indeed God is taken into consideration at all. *He,* the personal God of the Bible, has been changed into a "That," and fitted into the "system Es." God becomes the progressive in man and man's faith is "an acceptance of the inborn progressive tendencies."[9] And on the basis of this new conception of God and man, the new psychology intends to justify the evangelical meaning of "sola gratia," "sola fide," "by grace alone," "by faith alone." Müller-Braunschweig writes: "Previously we defined 'That' as the quintescence of elemental emotion drives. This definition does not

147

completely characterize the 'That.' To be sure, the elemental emotion drives belong to the 'That.' But 'That' means more; it is similar to the unconscious aspect of the ego and superego. It is the mother country, the undifferentiated matrix, of the psychical total ego, out of which, through states of evolution, phases of the ego and superego have been later differentiated. On the basis of these deliberations, it should be obvious to us that the most important reference for our life is neither the ego, nor the superego, but 'That.' This insight is in agreement with that of religion, namely, that the life conditioned by an outside 'ought' is not a life rooted in the innermost, and that there is something more inclusive than the 'ought.' Psychoanalytically speaking, this is the 'That.' In the unconscious, in the 'That' alone, in the final analysis lie the possibilities for transformation and realignment and the creating forces by means of which a new personal life may arise. This creating force is identical to what psychoanalysis includes under the concept libido."[10] In a turbid "Mutterboden" of the instincts, the higher and the lower are thrown together into one mass of energy, and above this "system Es" is placed the rubric: Libido, charitas, gratia. Roman Catholic Christianity, with its "gratia infusa" would profit by an investigation as to whether or not it has something in common with this sort of "religious" cogitation; it is certain that there is no relationship between this and the personal concept of God found in evangelical Christianity.

NOTES AND REFERENCES

[1] Pfister: *Die psychanalytische Methode*, p. 273.

[2] Reference is not found in the original text (that is, in Runestam's text).

[3] *Ges. Schriften*, Vol. VI, p. 286 ff.

[4] Franz Alexander depicts the case as follows: "The prime sublimation of the sex drive consists in this that a finer (zärtlich) component separates itself from the sensual sexuality. This finer component is the foundation for the building of the family in that it serves to neutralize the hatred for the father. This event indicates the conquering of the Oedipus Complex, and is the first step toward community structure. The desexualized love later extends from the father to the brother community, and thus leads to the building of the state." *Die Psychoanalyse der Gesamtpersönlichkeit*, p. 224.

[5] *Psychoanalyse der Gesamtpersönlichkeit*, p. 27 ff.

[6] *Ges. Schriften*, Vol. VI, p. 380.

[7] How grossly materialistic and unpsychological in this connection they have been in the field of psychoanalysis is evidenced by an expression from the previously cited writer, Alexander: "The amount of eros drive necessary to neutralize the hatred for the father is taken from the sensual genital yearning for the mother, this yearning being desexualized or expressed otherwise and sublimated into a spiritualized (zärtlich) attachment. As we have already mentioned, sublimation means a decrease of intensity, a diluting of the erotic components, when with the same quantitative libido not only the mother but also the father together become objects of sublimated (zärtlich) love." (*Psychoanal. der Gersamtpersönlichkeit*, p. 225).

[8] Nathan Soderblom: *Kristenhetens möte i Stockholm*, p. 433.

[9] Geijerstam: *Zeitschr, f. Psychotherapie*, p. 85.

[10] *Arzt u. Seelsorger*, Vol. II, p. 61.

IX

INDIVIDUAL PSYCHOLOGY

THE TENDENCY IN psychology that I have thus far discussed is essentially the Freudian tendency and that of the psychoanalysts closely associated with his thinking. However, over against the strictly Freudian point of view, there are several more or less independent movements, one of which has attracted attention and interest, and which, according to my judgment, deserves consideration on the part of Christian theology as well as of the Christian ethic. This movement has its impetus in men such as Alfred Adler and C. G. Jung.

That which differentiates Adler with his individual psychology, and Jung with his analytical psychology, from Freud is to be found in their differing ideal of the *content* of the "life energy." From the difference at this juncture follow all the variations from Freud in logical order.

In Adler and his school of thought, the psychological theory behind the practice of psychotherapy presents a picture quite different from that of Freud. Individual psychology is set up to discover something in the patient quite different from what the psychoanalyst appears to find, even though the therapeutic methodology remains the same. The analyst is on the trail of the sex drive and its maladjustments. Individual psychology attaches importance to the feeling of inferiority, and appears to find in this a hidden aspiration to power or "Geltungsbedürfnis." In comparing Freud and Adler, this is the one thing that marks the striking difference between them: where the one emphasizes the insistent sexual demand of the libido, the other accentuates the desire for power and self-importance.

As set forth in his *Studie über die Minderwertigkeit von Organen,* the situation is as follows, according to Adler: Weakness in certain organic systems have the tendency to *compensate* for this weakness or inferiority by means of exercise and training, a tendency which easily leads to overcompensation. Adler's whole psychological scheme rests upon this observation, and on this he bases his theory about neurosis. The neurotic person is put into a position where he must compensate for his shortcoming, and in the process of so doing he goes too far; that is, he "overcompensates." But this status is not peculiar to the definitely nervous person. Moreover, it is not merely something to be attributed to those afflicted with some organic defect. The fact of the matter is that it is a situation in which mankind in general finds itself. Man's status from the start is such that he is forced into this position. He enters this world as a weak and helpless being and becomes subject to the protection and care of others. He finds himself from the start in the position of one who is weak and inferior, and thus from the very beginning he is forced to consider himself as inferior. Thus man in general is actually predestined to a position of "compensation" or to a feeling of inferiority which with psychological necessity implies an intensification of the need for the feeling of being somebody, or a sense of self-importance. The implication is that from this point of view this is man's basic need; it is an expression of man's will to live, his desire for personal existence; it is his "will to power." Man wants to be *something* for himself and to have a meaning and significance as the individual that he actually is.

But this "will to power" which accordingly constitutes man becomes highly stimulated in some persons because the feeling of inferiority in them is for some reason or other more pronounced. The more marked the sense of inferiority is, the more intensified will be the need to demonstrate for oneself and others that this feeling and the state which accompanies this feeling are false. And thus compensation and overcompensation set to work, using every means at their disposal, conscious as well as unconscious, in order to reach the goal: the victory of the will to power, self-realization, and superiority. Instinctively and with purpose—often with subconscious purposefulness—the person inflicted with the feeling of inferiority outlines for himself a plan for life in which the guiding principle is the will to power, to superiority, and to security. This will to power need not necessarily be aggressive and take the offensive over against life, the objective world, other persons, or one's mission. Most frequently it is rather passive, evasive, and defensive. As a rule it does not dare to make an open attack in its struggle for self-realization, but makes its approach in the manner of the weakling; it does not by force raise itself above the stronger, nor does it seek in a positive manner to conquer and subdue the environment, but by means of disdaining the strong, and vanquishing him by subtle craftiness, a phantom victory is achieved to assuage the demand for power. No one becomes a greater tyrant than the weakling, the sickly, the nervous person who understands and has the ability to use his environment in order to achieve cherished power through which content is given to an otherwise negative and empty view of life. And no one allows himself to be the inconsiderate recipient of services of all kinds, as if he were a lord so much as he who evades the opportunity for services which are offered by the tasks that rise up to challenge him.

This negative attitude and *modus operandi* of the will to power is actually of necessity dictated by the lack of courage and self-confidence or an inadequate "faith," qualities which are the chief characteristics of a sense of inferiority and which it is the responsibility of analysis to remove and to replace them with courage and confidence. As already indicated, this lack of courage actually besets every person to the extent that each one from the start has been subjected to the status of inferiority. As a matter of course, some persons are born into this world with special handicaps, not so much because of weaker mental equipment, but rather because of certain organic inferiority, and primarily because they happen to come into an unsuitable environment for general development, and also because of the loveless and unreasonable rearing by which they may be victimized. On account of this many develop from the very start a strong feeling of inferiority, and from the earliest years, unreflectingly or with definite calculation, as the logic of the situation and as the guiding principle of self-realization forces them, they begin to formulate a plan for life which will be of service in their struggle for power and superiority. It is among these that "nervousness" finds its victims. Nervousness is the offspring of the inferiority feeling and the "Geltungsbedürfnis" which seeks to make up for the lack, due to feelings of inferiority, by means of overcompensation. And nervousness is fed and nurtured by the insufferable tension of this mental attitude.

154

But other maladjustments ensue. The nervous person is of necessity an egoist. As such he prefers to carry on his struggle for self-realization along negative lines; that is to say, he prefers not to be aggressive, but would rather achieve his mission in life in a cautious and evasive manner. He does not dare to assume the risk of defeat, which might result in an intensification of the feeling of inferiority. Consequently he evades current duties, or he avoids making a decision for or against a given obligation. In this manner he isolates himself more and more from social relationships and from the actual determinants of his own life. Later we shall return to the moral implications of this nervous distress.

For the moment it is of primary importance to "pin point" Adler's position in its relation to Freud's conception of "life energy," that is to say, to Freud's sex theory and to his doctrine of repression. As far as the theories of Adler are concerned, sex does have an important role in man's life, but he does not make sex a basically constitutive part or basic force in man. Rather, according to Adler, sexual life is used in the struggle for power and superiority, having a subordinate position in this struggle, however. In some aspects of this struggle for self-realization, the sexual life assumes considerable importance. The will to "manliness" in contrast to the weak and inferior femininity, a notion which is part of the ideal of the struggle for power—the so-called "masculine protest"—is evidence that the will to power would enhance itself also in this sphere. The inferior person desires to prove himself superior even in the area of the erotic and sexual. On the surface it would appear as if the sex drive were dictating the aims and objectives, while as a matter of fact, its struggle for satisfaction is only a constituent part of the inferior person's chief objective, namely, to enhance his desire for superiority.

Consequently nervousness cannot be said to be grounded in any repression into the unconscious of the desire of the sex drive, where the insisting, illegitimate demands of this drive would remain as a threat. First and foremost it is quite impossible here, according to the teachings of Adler, to draw any clear line of demarcation between the conscious and the unconscious. Moreover, the repression into the unconscious is, according to Adler, rather a consequence than a cause of the attitude toward life that brings about neuroses. Repression is, namely, one of the means employed by self-enhancement and the will to power for purposes of achieving the goal. Because the course of life and its guiding principles laid down by the will to power are made unconscious, they become more inaccessible and more difficult to discover, and are therefore able all the more successfully to continue their function, that is, to intensify the nervousness.

The situation is this: While, according to Freud, nervousness has its root in the frustration of a drive which has the perfect right to assert itself before all other forces of life, according to Adler, nervousness has its root in a drive or struggle within man, the status of which, in the form forced upon it through the feeling of inferiority, is highly doubtful, not to say illegitimate. The differentiation just made becomes the focal point in consideration of the moral qualities involved in the view of Adler as compared to that of Freud.

In general, the methodology of soul healing used by individual psychology is essentially the same as that used by psychoanalysis. It (individual psychology) employs intensified phantasies and dreams in order to get on the track of the nervous person's "life-plan" and unconscious or undiscovered guiding principles or inner "compunctions." But, of course, here as well as in the Freudian psychoanalysis, the very procedure itself determines largely what one *expects* to find; that is to say, the particular theory as to what constitutes the basic driving force determines the findings. If the analyst proceeds from the assumption that this force is the sex drive he will, of course, primarily look for this and interpret everything accordingly; if, on the other hand, he proceeds on the assumption that the basic drive is the struggle for power and self-realization, then the characteristic expressions of the patient, expressions useful to the analyst, are noted with the intention of tracking down this drive and its individual manifestations. Obviously these varying approaches imply far-reaching differentiations, particularly in reference to the interpretation of dreams.

Before I treat this point in the comparison between Freud and Adler, a point which must finally become decisive as these views are placed in the light of Christianity, I shall give a brief consideration to C. G. Jung's analytical psychology. This psychology is characterized primarily by its attack on the onsesidedness in the theories of both Freud and Adler concerning the basic forces of the soul, that is, Freud's emphasis on sex, and Adler's emphasis on the will to power. According to Jung the soul is much more complex than these theories would indicate. Jung is, like Adler, teleologically oriented in his psychology; by this is meant that he does not, in the first place, ask for the causes of illness in terms of the past, but according to the determination, the meaning, and the construction of the new life and the resolving of the conflict *in terms of the present*. This determines his total psychotherapeutic procedure. "I consider," says he, "the groping in the past for reportable specific causes for illness both as a waste of time and as a misleading prejudice, because neuroses, regardless of their genesis and the time at which they may

158

have arisen, are conditioned and supported by a constantly present improper attitude, an attitude which when once *discovered must be* corrected *today* and not in some infantile past."[1] "Further," he continues, "my view differs from that of Freud and Adler by the circumstance that my evaluation of the unconscious is essentially different from theirs . . . For me the unconscious is not simply a gathering place for all impure spirits or other odious vestiges from past experience, as, for example, the treasure of historical *opinion publique* which constitutes Freud's superego, but in its essential meaning it is the eternally living and creating source of origins which obviously uses old symbols but infuses them with a new meaning and a new spirit."[2]

In spite of these differences between Freud on the one hand and Adler on the other—differences which caused Jung to state that Adler not only theoretically, but also practically, differs to such a degree from the Freudian tendency in every essential that their common source is hardly discoverable any more—it might, nevertheless, be possible, from a decisive point of view,[3] to bring all three under the same heading, that is, in determining what nervousness is. It seems most difficult to unite Freud and Adler. As we have discovered, nervousness arises quite differently for these men. While the one ascribes it to a repressed or "confined" sex drive, the other sees its origin in the tension between the feeling of inferiority and its enforced struggle for power. These points of view seem to have nothing in common; in the one a drive is set forth, the sex drive or the love drive, with a justified claim to assert itself, and the checking of this drive by means of repression; in the other, a different drive is in the foreground; this is the drive toward self-realization, or the drive to *be of importance, to mean something;* and the unwarranted demands of this drive are accentuated. But, just because in the first case the drive (the sex drive) has a positive connotation, and the drive in the second case (the drive toward power and self-realization) *has a negative* connotation, the difference between these points of view is not so great as one would at first suppose.

Actually their relatedness may be easily seen in a glance at a drive which runs parallel to Adler's drive of self-realization, namely, the drive to fellowship and the surrender of selfishness. This drive is really never quite silenced. The sense of fellowship is an integrating aspect of human personality, according to Individual Psychology. It is not something that can be simply forced out by metaphysical command; the feeling for, or the devotion to, fellowship is a fact of life itself which must be considered as a force factor, however badly it may have been treated by the egocentric desire for power. In spite of everything man sustains a "Mut zur Hingabe und zur Selbstaufgabe des Ich."[4] It is, therefore, a reaction to life itself, to the repressed sense of fellowship and need for devotedness, when the egoist (the enhancer of the self) has to pay for his isolation from fellowship in terms of neuroses. Consequently, according to Adler's psychology, it may be said that the cause of the neuroses here is restrained "love drive," only that "love" at this point is not conceived in terms of "sexuality."

When Freud's and Adler's theories are thus simplified and made presentable, they become comparable and their points of similarity stand out clearly. First of all, we note a striking *formal* similarity between these points of view: in Freud the ego and superego with a negative connotation stand over against the love drive and the sex drive respectively; in Adler the isolating "ego will," or will to power, stands with a negative connotation against the "love drive" or the need for devotion to fellowship. In the case of both men the drive for devotedness holds a central position. Both have the opinion that through the liberated functions of the drive for devotedness—whether it expresses itself in sex drive or fellowship drive—the road will be open to free devotedness to other tasks of life. Therefore the whole problem will finally be concentrated on the question concerning the content of the devotion and to the question regarding the nature of the power or "ego drive" that would restrain the devotion.

In reference to the questions just posed, psychoanalysis and Individual Psychology are placed in quite different positions. The devotion drive and the "ego drive" respectively receive altogether different contents. "The ego" is given a negative evaluation in either camp; it is, or generally appears as, an evil that frustrates devotedness, "the good." But it is characteristic of psychoanalysis that the ego finds its best expression in the superego or the moral ego and its censor, while the ego in Individual Psychology represents self-realization, which does not demand any moral concepts of the ego but simply is intent upon a realization of its will to power. In Individual Psychology the "ego" is "the evil" because without consideration it would drive through to its goal, quite unconcerned about "fellowship"; "the ego" is evil for psychoanalysis because it would check the drive with which the *individual here and now* would enhance himself, namely, the libido. That the libido is also existing in sublimated form and can express itself not only as an egoistically insistent sex drive but also as real love or devotedness to fellowship in some form, is of secondary importance: "the ego" or the "superego" is given a negative connotation by psychoanalysis because it resists and hinders the egotistical pleasure-seeking libido, while "the ego" in

Individual Psychology gets its negative connotation because it resists and hinders the devotion to fellowship.

This decisive difference in the ego-function in psychoanalysis and Individual Psychology is really but an expression of the difference in the "devotion drive." In psychoanalysis it is an individual drive; in Individual Psychology it is a fellowship drive. In psychoanalysis it is the libido or sexuality; in Individual Psychology it has actually the characteristic of yielding to preoccupation with the ego and self-realization and thus a fellowship function. As a matter of fact, the relation between the isolated person and general fellowship constitutes the key to the theory of Individual Psychology. Its basic idea is that only he is healthy and sound whose life is rooted in fellowship. The sense of fellowship is part and parcel of man's life, and one must restrain onself in order to subdue this feeling, or else one must ignore its demands.[5] But every such violation is self-deceit. Every selfish person deceives himself.[6] Selfishness, egocentricity, makes him blind to reality, blind to objectivity, and at the same time it causes him to miss his own "infinite" goals.

Through these considerations it appears that Individual Psychology, which by its deviation from Freud's basic theory regarding life energy is happily liberated from the difficulties attending the notion of sublimation, at least on the surface approaches the Christian view in ethical matters. Here and there selfishness and lack of love oppose devotion to fellowship and self-sacrifice, and there is no doubt that here is present a relationship which it would be folly to deny or of which to rid oneself. *He* has not understood much of Christian ethics who cannot find a great deal to learn from Adler's Individual Psychology. If one wishes to see how Adler's psychology in its best formulations approaches, and partly coincides with, Christian ethical thinking, one may read Fritz Künkel's extraordinary work, *Einführung in die Charakterkunde auf individualpsychologischer Grundlage,* where Künkel, to be sure, steps beyond the bounds of the real or original Individual Psychology of Adler.

With the similarities just noted, it must, however, be said that Individual Psychology, in the form in which it is presented by Adler and the more circumscribed among his followers, is not congruent with Christian psychology and ethics. What is missing is the transcendental background for the psychological course of events and the teleological determination for man's life which gives the whole view the character of fictionalism or a "Philosophie of Als-Ob" (Philosophy of "As If"). The ultimate consequences of the tension between selfishness and devotedness have not been drawn, and to the extent that they have been drawn it has been in such a manner as to remove Individual Psychology greater distances from the areas of the Christian ethic.

Therefore when the preceding presentation has intimated how the tension between egoism and the feeling of fellowship, as presented by Individual Psychology, has its counterpart in the Christian psychological distinction between selfishness on the one hand and the life of devotedness of faith and love on the other, we have thus set before us a basic position of agreement between Christian ethics and Individual Psychology. However, it is necessary here to restrict the implications so as not to make Individual Psychology more Christian than it is or wishes to be. In previous statements it has been said that the "ego-function" or self-enhancement in Individual Psychology essentially has a negative connotation or indicates a disvalue, or an evil. This is quite correct, but essentially it obtains only in so far as self-enhancement through the inferiority complex has risen to an immeasurable height; otherwise, according to Individual Psychology, self-enhancement has its proper place. And in any case, even if it is empirically established that self-enhancement and devotedness are constantly in a state of tension in relation to each other, this tension is not normal, even if, from the point of view of development, this seems necessary. Because normality should mean that they keep each other in balance, or enter into a synthesis, both of these tendencies of life are neither conflicting nor mutually exclusive, as in the case of the principles of good and evil in a religious system. In the final analysis there is no *evil power* of any kind in the efforts of the ego to achieve "likeness to God." Similarly, there is no particular *good power* in devotion to fellowship. The matter is viewed "biologically" and is considered within the framework of life here and now. And if the consequences of this view are extended in a sociological direction, as is done by Adler and others, and is shown to favor socialism and its fight against the pathological enhancement of the ego of modern individualism, there is surely not in this notion any particular evidence of nearness to the Christian ethic.

That which differentiates Individual Psychology and its ethics from the Christian ethic is a curtailment of its ideal of individuality as well as its ideal of fellowship. Individual Psychology is satisfied with an ideal of personality that is too earth bound, just as it is satisfied with a similarly earth-bound fellowship. And this is bound up with the fact that it has not gone to the bottom of the matter in reference to the previously discussed tension between self-enhancement and self-sacrifice in their radical implications, nor arrived at the objective forces behind these human functions. It has not uncovered the radical evil of selfishness. It is not as if Christianity were a stranger to the notion of the peculiar stamp of individuality and in this sense not acquainted with "self-enhancement." But Christianity implies that *this* form of "self-enhancement," or the crystallization of individuality, is achieved, not by any halfway measures with the feeling of fellowship, but by a continually repeated victory at the very seat of the evil of selfishness; and this is to be achieved by devotion to a power which judges and restores and enables "a new man daily to come forth and rise."

NOTES AND REFERENCES

[1] According to my understanding, there is not at this point such a great deviation from Freud as Jung would have one believe, and the common notion in the literature that where Freud in his psychotherapeutic practice uses the word "Woher?" "from where?" Jung and Adler use the word "Wohin?" "where to?" is highly misleading. With Freud, as well as with the others, the "life stream" is, of course, directed forward, and the release is considered a liberation now and for the future, even if the causes for the conflict, which for the present continue to be unresolved, lie far back in time and demand an emotional journey of the memory back to the past.

[2] W. M. Kranfeld, *Die Psychoanalyse Einführingvon,* C. G. Jung, p. 12 f.

[3] Cf. supra., p. 6.

[4] Erwin Wexberg, *Individual Psychologie,* 1928, p. 81.

[5] Alfred Adler: *Individual Psychology,* pp. 28 and 118 f.

[6] Fritz Kunkel: *Einführung in die Characterkunde auf individualpsychologischer Grundlage,* second edition, 1929, p. 16 f.

X

RETROSPECT

THROUGHOUT THIS TREATISE it has not been my intention to maintain that psychoanalysis should be considered as of no consequence for psychotherapy. Such would be a contention quite contrary to obvious facts. The assignment I took upon myself at the very beginning was to clarify the line of demarcation between Christian and psychoanalytical psychology, and between Christian and psychoanalytical "salvation." I have especially directed myself against efforts to obfuscate this borderline, particularly where psychoanalysis has beclouded the issue by using Christian terminology. That Christian psychology and theology, not to speak of Christian ethics, according to my conception, have a great deal to learn from psychoanalysis has been clearly indicated. Whether or not, and to what extent, psychoanalysis can or should be used in the practical therapeutical relief of spiritual abnormality is, of course, a question of no immediate concern to theology and Christianity. That is a matter to be settled by the psychiatrist and the psychoanalyst. As I have stated above, Christian theology is not interested in concealing from itself the fact that there are mental ailments which Christian soul cure cannot treat or control; and among these are included such as are of a religio-moral nature without being primarily objects of Christian soul cure. To this category belong potent sin and guilt consciousness, which is apt to accompany melancholy. The Christian "Seel Sorger" should observe extreme caution that he does not assume capacities and powers beyond those granted him by his Christian faith and love, and the Christian office committed to him.

But from the preceding discussion another consideration has become obvious, namely, that no clear line can in every instance be drawn between the function of the psychiatrist and the pastor. Because of this difficulty, the analyst cannot be nonchalantly dismissed. It just so happens that analysis has without question discovered entree to levels in the human soul which place the relationship between religio-moral forces and psychic abnormalities in a new light. And if the pastor has been able or forced to look upon the physician and the psychiatrist as assistants in works of mercy, he ought not, without further consideration, decline corresponding assistance proffered by the psychoanalyst, if he is able to maintain the basic line of demarcation, a line which many analysts have tended to ignore.

As far as I am concerned, it is for the time being

an open question as to what extent psychoanalysis should be employed as an instrumental aid in Christian soul care. It is obvious, as has already been indicated, that there are situations in general soul cure where a certain amount of preparatory "roughing-in," in a sort of "psychological common labor" is needed, without which Christian soul care is helpless. Bodily ailments and material need, just as well as psychic conflicts, may set up better mental presuppositions for the breaking forth of a more profound spiritual life, but one does not for this reason permit the sufferer to go unassisted, if help is available. However, one must bear in mind that just as analysis can prepare and otherwise set the stage for a richer spiritual life, just as easily can it set up insurmountable barriers against its coming into being. As a matter of course, this applies somewhat to spiritual ailments. The closer these approach the nature of religio-moral conflicts, the more indeed must one be cautioned against seeking to alleviate them by mental release of energy in terms of psychoanalysis. But where the conflicts have so completely eclipsed the soul that the sun rays of grace cannot penetrate the darkness, there a psychic preparatory function is needed.

What value psychoanalysis can have as an instrumental aid in the performance of this preparatory "common labor," is for me an open question. But it does appear to me that it could be of considerable help if it is properly utilized by the Christian pastor. But the prerequisite is that the analyst should clear himself of some of the dogmas of psychoanalysis, and that he honestly permits analysis to become an aid instead of slipping away from its real purpose in the interest of psychological naturalism, oblivious to the most significant sources of power. Assuredly it is of great importance that the "Seel Sorger" should have an eye to the *natural* conditions involved in cases of illness, so that as occasion may demand he will be able to view the case in terms of cause and effect. Again we find, at this juncture, that psychoanalysis has made its contribution in that it has cleared up many areas hitherto confused or little understood. A word of caution, however: Simply because analysis finds natural causes, one must not be led to think that the natural cause is the whole story. It may very well be but a small part of the religio-ethical situation. This warning and caution may not seem out of place when one considers the possibility that psychoanalysis may become more and more important within the church and general pastoral care. In more realistic terms, the following consideration seems to be in order: it seems quite reasonable to imagine that a pastor may become so taken up by the practice of psychoanalysis as to relegate all mental and spiritual ailments to strictly endogenic physical causes and neglect his chief function as a Christian pastor. That is, there may be pastors who have had but little interest, and therefore little success, in general pastoral care. Such servants of the church may easily fall for what may seem to be a more objective and scientific procedure.

It is a serious matter under all conditions, if the analyst goes to work with preconceived notions, dogmatically bound to the idea that mental conflicts have a sexual basis and thus of necessity will lead the analysis in this direction, as is the case with the Freudian school. Sexuality is most assuredly such a force in man's life that it very frequently plays a role in conflicts, and intensifies the conflict, if it does not actually constitute its very center. It is, therefore, quite plausible that analysis can discover even this power factor. And it can, under certain conditions, be of value to the patient to have this facet of his life examined. But the seriousness is involved in this that psychoanalysis proceeding in the spirit of Freud is bent upon the resolving of conflicts in terms of the sex drive, and to consider this drive as the life force which more than any other force possesses the right of pristine life to live and to be re-enthroned. It can become ruinous for the patient who learns to view his life under this aspect and to turn his attention away from the real cause of his malady, which perchance is something quite different. Besides this, there is the possibility that the theory about sexuality as a basic force of life is dangerous even from this point of view that it sets up a philosophy of life and of necessity results in a looser morality, especially in relation to sex life, as has been indicated above.

By comparison, Adler's Individual Psychology, which everywhere traces the egoistic drive of self-enhancement, entails less risk. In part it looks upon this drive as a danger to the life of the patient; in part it seeks rather to revive in him the sense of the life of fellowship, the courage to meet life's obligations, and an objective mind, which releases from preoccupation with self; and which in part finally seeks to enable the patient, by forsaking a life motivated by selfishness, to apprehend a new philosophy of life which, where it is most profoundly understood, actually has a tendency to be oriented towards eternity, or as Spinoza would say it: view life "sub specie aeternitatis." In all of this Individual Psychology can find points of contact with the Christian view of life.

XI

PSYCHOANALYSIS AND CHRISTIAN
SOUL CARE

SOME TWENTY-FIVE YEARS have elapsed since the earlier editions of this book. As I look back on this work, and consider the developments during these years, I sense that there are several questions aimed at me, and these questions I feel obligated to answer.

In the first place, I find a most pressing need for a more direct and more pointed inquiry than was made in the foregoing chapters concerning the function and meaning of psychoanalysis in the general field of soul care. Moreover, in this connection I shall seek to clarify what essentially differentiates the Christian concept of the soul from that of the psychoanalytical. In a sense this will be a summarizing review, but a review in which some rather embarrassing questions will come to the fore; questions regarding actual weaknesses in Christian soul care and the necessity of greater clarity in, and a stronger grasp of, the theory and practice of Christian soul care.

Questions of this nature will arise: Has Christian

soul care had greater success than has psychotherapy? Has it had better results? Has it been more effective? Or does Christian soul care perhaps consciously shy away from such "results"? If this be the case, why is it? Does the "church" actually seek to avoid the radical interference with man's psyche which is characteristic of psychoanalysis? Does the church give up in the presence of the difficulties seen by the psychoanalysts, or does it intend to solve these problems in some other way, or will it perhaps not have to deal with these problems at all? What is actually the place and significance of *salvation* in soul care? Is salvation something that may be compared with the resolute psychoanalytic intervention in the sick and divided soul, healing it here and now; or is it merely, "in hope you are saved," that is, hope in an eventual liberation some time in eternity?

Obviously, these questions cannot be answered exhaustively. But what can be done here is to point out the status and problematic position in which soul care finds itself today; that is, point out the enormous, ever-widening obligations confronting soul care and the necessity for being organized and co-ordinated in a larger context, comparable to that of general psychotherapy.

The first and most pressingly urgent matter, as psychoanalysis and soul care are set side by side for purposes of comparison, is this: What is it that should be investigated as the comparison is made? The question is not whether or not psychology, or even psychoanalysis, should be used in soul care. It is, of course, self-evident that soul care, in some sense, uses psychology and practices psychoanalysis, since it is the soul, the psyche, which is to be helped, and in order to be helped must be subjected to the proper diagnosis. But right here one must inquire as to what sort of psychology is to be used in order to know the soul and direct the diagnosis. That is, is the psychology of the kind that can really approach the soul and objectively reflect and interpret its inner content? Or does it misinterpret the object it is supposed to portray?

My chief objection to the *modus operandi* of psychoanlysis is that it is based on a faulty and shallow psychology with its superficial notion of man's nature, and this in spite of its vaunted depth analysis. And the help it affords will be such as might be expected, even if at certain times and in certain respects it intervenes in a drastic manner.

This is not to deny that in psychoanalysis as well as in other psychotherapy one may make numerous correct observations and discover, under similar assumptions, a certain regularity in the appearance of congeries of complexes, inhibitions, and schizophrenic tendencies. One may even be able to aid in the resolving of these without sensing or dealing with the soul in terms of its real depth. And it is such partial discoveries about the soul, however correct, that bring about a great deal of misunderstanding here and there. Even within Christian camps one can find a dizzy ecstasy over psychology and psychoanalysis with the proclamation that Christian soul care will please oblige by taking heed to, and being guided by, the findings of psychology. (Somewhere) I have read: "In so far as psychology is a science, it is futile for the church to do otherwise than to interpret the gospel according to the new situation which has come about through this new knowledge about man." This is capitulation in the presence of psychology—all the schools of which lay claim to being a science in that they correctly portray reality—a capitulation which causes the evangelical interpretation of man to step aside in favor of modern psychology and in so doing questions the validity of Christian salvation itself. The author just quoted appears to infer—he himself uses the metaphor—that just as impossible as it is to hold to the Biblical view of the world at large, so it is impossible to follow the New Testament conception of man and of what is in man. From such reasoning it should be clear that one is not fully aware of the implication of what is being said. It would mean this: To the extent Jesus was ignorant of our new view of the world, so He was confused in reference to what is in man. In theological radicalism one cannot go much further. The gospel builds upon a definite conception of man, who he is, what is wrong with him, and what it is intended that he shall become. To set forth some other "modern" conception of man as the correct one, is to recommend a salvation different from that of the Christian. The very history of psychology, which shows how it vacillates between a Christian notion of man and the man portrayed in modern literature, or any other conceivable view of man, ought to give one pause before doing obeisance to one or the other of the schools of psychology.

Therefore one has every reason for taking care when a given psychology comes to the fore and proffers its services to Christian soul cure. What kind of psychology or what psychological direction should the church use? Freudians, who unconditionally interpret the course and conflict of the soul in terms of the proper or faulty adjustment of the sex drive? Adlerians, who see the soul's deepest secret in the will to power? Or psychologists of the school which in its formula for salvation calls upon the self-healing powers of the soul? Or, again, psychologists with some other theory of powers and drives which constitute the essence of the soul and its varied activity? One must not, in one's admiration for particlar insights, however correct, within the various psychologies overlook the fact that each school with its peculiar outlook and insights varies in its interpretations as to the very essence of the

human soul, and that each seeks to effect psycho-
therapic cure accordingly.

Over against this clamor of many and conflicting
interpretations and practices stands the New Testament with its own anthropology and psychology. It
is God's Law and God's Gospel. It unveils who man
is. All other psychologies by comparison become
psychologies of superficiality, however much they
may lay claim to being "depth psychology."

Christian soul care is, of course, aided by a psychological outlook, by psychological observations,
and psychological studies of the nature of man, and
especially his soul. Whether or not these psychological pursuits call themselves scientific is of little
import. And Christian soul care may learn a great
deal from psychoanalysis. Moreover, one ought to
rejoice whenever modern psychology gives evidence
of approaching the Christian outlook. But the
warning will bear repetition: One must not lose
one's head in adoration of psychology as such, simply because in various areas it does make many
valuable observations, observations which may be
of use in Christian soul care. In any case, what
must not be lost sight of is that, as far as Christian
soul care is concerned, it is decisively important that
the basic Christian concept of man and of what
Jesus Christ intends for man shall be constantly
kept in view.

Christ intends salvation. We shall never have

done with this concept. The term "salvation" has meaning and intents far beyond anything we can see at a glance. It encompasses time and eternity. It is not merely the quieting of an uneasy feeling; it also involves stirring and turmoil of the very depths. God's salvation is not simply peace; it is strife and agony. It quite disregards the insistence on harmony of soul. When salvation is peace, it is peace on a deep level, brought to life and reality in struggle. If salvation is worship, it is worship with sword in hand. And, beyond this, all the while the final salvation lies in the future, in eternity, when the strife is at an end and the crown is won. Salvation belongs to eternity; but it is also conversion here and now, conversion to both struggle and rest on the side of Christ, against destructive forces, against forces of lovelessness and unbelief, forces which destroy life, my life and that of others, and which would destroy peace within us and in our fellowship with man, and shut us out from heaven itself and from our eternity with God.

All Christian soul care aims, in the final analysis, at bringing the soul to Christ and into discipleship with Him, with all of its implications: security, confidence, assurance, willingness to surrender oneself to His service, to anxiety, struggle, and a continuing fight against temptations. All Christian soul care bears salvation in its hands, even if at times it is concealed from him who is being sought by it.

Whenever a Christian pastor approaches a person with the help he would bring, it is always done with attention to the soul. He views that person's soul as an arena for struggling forces. From the human point of view, the soul appears to be a football, tossed forth and back by opposing powers, that of God and that of the enemy of God. Therefore it cannot be limited to what it is for the moment, or to what it is now observed to be. It is in a status of relationship; it is directional, it is intentional,[1] or looked at from another point of view, it is something in the clutch of another. Thus it is something above and beyond what it is at the present.

It (the soul) is engaged by God, or else it is engaged by that servant of God's enemy called *the self*. It is not a limited quantum of energy; it is a directional motion, but not a directional motion once and forever fixed. For this reason, the salvation of the soul is a conversion, and a conversion to the proper direction of activity, the right attitude and the right faith. In its earthly existence the soul continues to remain in the hands of dual possibility. Consequently, salvation is of necessity a struggle between opposing forces. At best it alternates between peace and struggle, between rest and forced marches, between worship and onslaught.

Christian soul care never considers its task as a matter of regrouping or reorganizing of forces already present in the soul with some sort of intrapsychic liberation by the aid of a competent technician. It counts on a power from the outside, from Him who has hold of the soul, that is, from God. The soul is never merely "itself."

Consequently it may be said: Christian soul care depends on a psychology which is not merely psychology. It is a psychology which maintains an open view, upward, outward, inward, toward a "thou," toward a source of inspiration. In *rapport* with this objective force, the soul becomes enlarged. It does not become limited to the magnitude and function which now is the "soul." In its tendency to go beyond its present status the soul receives a new indefiniteness with which a purely psychological reflection without God (and His enemy) cannot deal. It is something indefinite with possibilities which point beyond the possible.

In this way Christian soul care always includes much more than does psychoanalysis. It reckons with the powers beyond the soul, powers that fight for the soul. This sort of background is ever present in Christian soul care. It is a matter of concern ever to seek to enlist God's power on behalf of the soul, to awaken it, to jolt it to its senses, to bring about its surrender at God's mercy, to deliver it from forces of destruction and to reawaken it to a new conception of a vitalized peace. This awakening and comforting is brought about by God's law and gospel, and a harmony between the two.

These are the means by which God gets His grasp on the soul and by which He seeks to maintain it. It cannot be accomplished by just one or the other; it must be both law and gospel. The law prevents love from becoming a cheap experience of God's love which is not love. Ontologically speaking, God is *not* love. On the other hand, the gospel, which speaks of the Son of God on the cross and of what it costs God to love man, makes it difficult for the law to set up a do-it-yourself morality. Thus, it becomes the task of Christian soul care to bring the law and the gospel of God to human souls.

It is granted, of course, that there is nothing standing in the way of the psychoanalyst's having the same goal in view. That is, he may take Christian soul care into consideration and deal with the soul with this background in mind, and thus make use of these extra-human resources. In this manner he will have subordinated his psychoanalysis to Christian soul cure and thus will have broadened his psychology. That psychoanalysis so employed is of great worth there can be no doubt.

It is not a mere accident that Christian psychoanalysis has begun to operate side by side with what is ordinarily thought of as Christian soul care, or at least that they are beginning to go hand in hand. Here, however, we arrive at a point where a great difference between psychoanalysis and Christian soul care becomes obvious as they are compared. This is it: In individual soul care as practiced in our churches there is a great lack, if not a total absence, of anything that may be psychoanalysis. Even the confessional does not function in any sense comparable to psychoanalysis. Moreover, private soul care in the congregations has been reduced to a minimum and generally limits itself to pastorally directed conversations without coming to grips with the matter in any profound manner. Christian activity operates in quite another direction. It has become *proclamation*, preaching.

We find, then, a difference in the very operational structure, the very concept of the respective missions of psychoanalysis and Christianity. In its function Christianity most certainly includes soul care. But many have the notion that this soul care is essentially and primarily a proclamation. And perhaps there are Christian leaders who would actually warn us against any preoccupation with soul care, because it would call undue attention to the soul as such. Real soul care, so it is inferred, rather concerns itself with the freeing of persons from their preoccupation with the self, a malady which is encouraged or induced by personal soul care. God, Christ, the Word, and not the *soul*, must hold the center of the stage, it is argued.

Obviously this touches upon a very serious problem confronting the church. The church has been commissioned to make God's love a vital reality in the world and thus to care for the souls of men. Now, the church proposes to accomplish this by means of the *proclamation,* the "message"! It is apparent to everyone that here the church has failed most miserably. Could it be that for the sake of the proclamation the church has neglected soul care? Perhaps the road to the human heart—the road of the "message"— must go by way of (individual) soul care. I am quite convinced that this must be the *modus operandi.* I believe that the total operational activity of the church must be oriented in the direction of soul care in a manner quite different from present practices. The proclamation, yes, even theology, must learn to apprehend, and be conditioned by, the mission of soul care exemplified by Jesus Christ himself. This is an issue of paramount importance in these dire times.

Among the several facets of the situation in which modern man finds himself there are two which especially appear to characterize man in the context in which the present inquiry is moving: Man breathes the air of doubt, and wages a terrific fight against agnosticism and unbelief; the other is this, that man has been left in isolation, without authority in spiritual matters as never before in history. Both of these factors co-operate in a most gruesome fashion to bring about the destruction of man's faith and spiritual existence. The individual has had "to become his own pope and church," to use Luther's phrase. A radical democracy in matters spiritual has thus led us to this state of affairs. There is no authority guiding faith; there is no authority over against emancipated modern man, an emancipation, by the way, which in and of itself has brought ennui, dismay, and suffering. In former days the church served to unify its members. There was a collective unity in which soul care was exercised and in which the individual could enter as a rather happily unemancipated part. Today this collectivity has disintegrated and the individual stands quite alone, emancipated, unhappy, and withal unable to help himself spiritually. This person really is in need of soul care. It is toward such a person that soul care must primarily be directed. It is his predicament which is repeated time and time again in each case of individual soul care. That is, this individual who in his agony of soul cries out for help for his specific need is involved in the same distressed state, with the same inability to believe, that is characteristic of all.

This state of affairs is a problem of our time, and is a problem which psychotherapy does not know. Present-day soul care does not have at its disposal the socially recognized and spiritually rich apperceptive mass that it once had. To be sure, one may approach whoever appears to be in need, with one's soul care, but not in the same clear-cut manner, nor with the presuppositions as before. Doubt and timidity have entered in, bringing about embarrassment and anxiety, threatening to destroy or make banal the delicate relationship between the pastor and the one seeking his help. This is the way, then, the way to the individual that the church must make and follow, if it would accomplish Christ's saving mission. It is the way through the darkness of unbelief. And this way through doubt and unbelief is one which the pastor must clearly understand is also his way and one he must traverse oftener than he may be willing to admit, if he is to be able to bring succor to unhappy and distressed souls. In this manner he will be in a position to sense that seemingly simple difficulties have their roots rather deep, and apparently mundane problems will be seen to have spiritual implications. More often than not it will be seen that one must resort to the basic Christian formula: "Help thou mine unbelief." In general: Christian soul care must never forget that its chief mission is to bring to mankind this gift of love: *help to believe*.

But the objection may be made: Surely it cannot be of great importance whether or not one *labels* help for the soul *Christian* or not; the main thing is that one brings aid, and approaches the needy person with the necessary love and sympathy. A great deal of Christian soul care has been practiced and is being practiced. Christ does not in a niggardly fashion ask whether or not the practitioner comes in His name. The matter of chief importance is that help is brought and that love has been shown. Social welfare, sponsored by society at large, bringing financial aid as well as other assistance, may very well also bring soul care to the afflicted. And there may even be a difference of opinion as to who actually brings the better soul care: the pastor who on behalf of his office reads the Word of God to him for whom he is to care, or the social worker who cares for the material welfare of the needy and his family.

The Father of our Lord Jesus Christ most assuredly has many such channels for the flow of His love to mankind. In this sense there is a far-reaching care exercised over man, including soul care, that is more inclusive than that exercised by the agency of the church. But, just as it is true that among all of the acts of love shown by the church it is its special obligation to open heaven to the children of distress, so it is also true that there is no sense in talking about Christian soul care where the message of salvation is omitted and where salvation is not the very essence of the help given.

There may be occasions when the pastor may be tempted to say nothing about religion or Christianity, or more specifically, Christ's special mission of love to mankind, that is, salvation. And most certainly are there instances where such silence is indicated as the better part of wisdom. Or again, there may be situations where there appears to be no justification for speaking of the soul and God, etc., either because it is not necessary or because it would be hopeless in any event. But soul care it is, or can be, by implication even though one may be dealing with everyday mundane problems and conflicts.

A pastor's mediating activity in marriage problems may be a case in point. This service may be rendered, and is probably usually rendered, without any specific Christian reference. One may admonish and give sound advice as one seeks to inject rime and reason into the situation. One need not necessarily interpose something obviously *Christian* in order to inquire into the causes and other factors involved in the marital conflict. The pastor would and should act like any other person put into a similar position. Often nothing extraordinary is required. But in the resolving of many marital difficulties pastoral soul care becomes paramount. In innumerable cases nothing short of Christian soul care avails. Christian salvation as such must enter in to give the parties in the conflict a new perspective, new values and a revaluation of older values. If ever confession is good for the soul, it is definitely an asset here.

Marital conflicts are patently due to failures, failures on the part of one or the other, and usually of both. Accusations, complaints, and countercomplaints tend to vanish under the impact of mutual confession and forgiveness. Moreover, he who is the mediator in this conflict, if he knows the way of confession and divine forgiveness, can with assurance direct the resolving of the conflict so that not only mutual forgiveness, but forgiveness from on high is achieved. In this manner Christ's mission to man becomes a reality and yields blessings far beyond the mere resolving of mundane marriage problems. Furthermore, the practice of soul cure at this juncture may have other implications. It could be that the incompatibility of the parties involved is of such a nature that no insight, however profound, and no adjustment, however great, can remove it. The dream of the bliss of mutual happiness did not become a reality and is not even a dream any more. But through pastoral soul care another vista may be opened. The new insights and the God-given new values may enable husband and wife to make revaluations to a degree that life together can be not only tolerable but actually worth while. Radically new perspectives can work wonders. And nothing is more radical, and no perspective more novel, than man's divine reorientation. When the kingdom of God comes into a person's life, the kingdom of this world is no longer a kingdom. This is not an injustice to the world; it never was a kingdom in fact, but merely an extravagant fiction.

Likewise, in marriage. Much of the unhappiness in marital life is due to extravagant presuppositions; fictions of beauty, love, perfection, and the most extravagant fiction of all: the right to happiness. But whatever the cause, real or imaginary, for marital friction and conflict, a vision of eternal values will reduce the values of this world to their proper size and relative importance. The *great faith*, faith in God and the things of God, will tend to bring about a sounder faith in the things of this world; that is, a realistic faith fully aware of the relativity of all mundane values. Disappointments will be reduced to a minimum because one has been made wise enough not to look for the ideal or for perfection. Christian soul care can do much to bring about such an outlook in all areas of human life. This, then, is the task of Christian soul care: to bring God and man together.

But this soul care faces mammoth problems. The chief difficulty lies in this, that in our day we are involved in doubt and unbelief as never before. And since Christian soul care moves and has its being in the field of faith, it is patent that general disbelief and doubt make the ground rather uncertain, to say the least. And, as has already been made clear, since persons have become isolated, individualized, personal soul care has become a necessity. The pastor must approach the individual in terms of his particular predicament and special problems, and gradually, step by step, and point by point, seek to overcome his doubt and to generate faith in him. Moreover, Christian soul care operates along a front enormously wide as compared with that of psychotherapy. It is involved in a much greater need and intensive assistance than that of psychoanalysis. It is because of this that any comparison between the two can never be satisfactory. It is vain to compare the results of soul care in one with the other, in order to mark differences in effectiveness. These two are doing radically different jobs.

My presentation resolves itself into a breakdown of the framework set up by tendencies to compare the work of Christian soul care with that of psychoanalysis. My aim is to point out a new and tremendous task that confronts the church of today. In a more conscious manner than hitherto the church must assume the task of personal work, individual soul care, as part and parcel of its working program. At the same time it must broaden its mission so as to become effective throughout the church in terms of soul care and not in terms of theology or preaching proclamation. The result should be that by means of this personal approach the individual be so conditioned that when he does hear the Word, that is, the proclamation, he shall apply it to himself and his needs. To this end a new and more realistic understanding of man, and a greater solicitude for his welfare, is demanded of the pastor. It is, of course, paramount that an intimate relationship, born of mutual trust and confidence, be achieved and maintained.

Who is in need of Christian soul care? Just a few who are in an especially bad way? Hard pressed cases that come under the treatment of psychotherapy? Yes, these, of course. But, as a matter of fact, all of us are proper objects of soul care. And not just because of some inherited evil or guilt, but because of our own personal involvement in the epidemic around us, man's real sin, unbelief.

A full realization of what is here implied confronts the doctrine of Christian soul care with a tremendous task. The solution is not to be found in the setting up of a method or practice as a counterpart or substitute for psychoanalysis or psychotherapy, intended for special cases in dire need of help. Naturally these special cases will not be overlooked, but the care set up for these particularly difficult cases must be so conceived as to be applicable in the larger context—to general soul care. Moreover Christian care must guard against becoming a mere competitor among other saving cures which tend to become mere therapy and to be preoccupied with "technique." It must not be satisfied with the giving of advice, comforting words, aid of one kind or another, which may be imparted to any and all without reference to Christ.

Christian soul care must be universally applicable to all stages and levels of need, for the dire and utterly abject cases, and to the everyday needs of ordinary people in all walks of life. This must be so because it comes not with temporary aid for temporary needs only; it comes with Christian salvation: faith, conversion, a revaluation of values. It places man in a new situation in life and makes him fit for that new life. Heaven itself must be made to hover over this personal, individual soul need, and heart and mind must be raised to its height and glory. Pain, suffering, and calamity will diminish in importance when the sufferer "beholds the kingdom of God." This is the essence of Christian soul care: To help the soul find the proper proportions and the right perspective in life by placing Jesus Christ and His kingdom in the center of the picture, and then allowing each one of us to be included as those who are attracted by Him to His cross, as well as blessed by Him who conquered on the cross.

NOTES AND REFERENCES

[1] Swedish usage of the term "intentional" here implies something more realistic than the Latin *ens intentionale*. It means also more than "design." It is something *in the hands of a designer,* moulder, director, etc.